R.A.C.E. for Greatness

R.A.C.E. for Greatness

From Relentless Pursuit to Million-Dollar Mastery: A Tactical Blueprint for Those Who Start with Nothing but Dream of Everything

Anthony J. Lee

Published by Game Changer Publishing

Paperback ISBN: 978-1-962656-77-1
Hardcover ISBN: 978-1-962656-78-8
Digital: ISBN: 978-1-962656-79-5

www.GameChangerPublishing.com

DEDICATION

For the Best Mother in the World, Arenia Lee,
you have made me who I am today!

Without you, this would never have been possible.

I Love You, thank you for everything.

Your Son,

~Anthony

Read This First

Just to say thanks for buying and reading my book, I would like to give you a few free bonus gifts, no strings attached!

To Download Your Free Gifts, Scan the QR Code:

R.A.C.E. for Greatness

From Relentless Pursuit to Million-Dollar Mastery:
A Tactical Blueprint for Those Who Start with
Nothing but Dream of Everything

Anthony J. Lee

www.GameChangerPublishing.com

Foreword

The world has changed a lot in recent years, and this new reality demands new ways of thinking.

That's why I'm honored to support my friend Anthony Lee and this book, *R.A.C.E. for Greatness.*

R.A.C.E. (Relentless, Attack, Connection, Execution) is a perfect acronym and simple way to focus on the essential tools and tactics to help you win whatever "race" you're running in life. What was once a long marathon to build a business or a career has now been changed and has become a series of 100-yard dashes. Speed matters. Sustained intensity matters. Most of all, results are more important than ever because the world is a less forgiving place than ever.

How many of these races are you going to win? More importantly, how will you train so that you'll cross the finish line first and become one of the 1% of people who live extraordinary lives?

Anthony has run countless important races and knows what it takes to win because that's exactly what he has done. Starting with nothing, he now owns several businesses and is the CEO of one of America's fastest-growing and largest privately held companies.

While success has greeted him at the finish line many times, his is a story about how he ran those races and what you should do to win, too.

Anthony knows how to fight and win battles because he's been doing it all his life.

He started in the trenches, learning how to fight his own battles as a poor mixed-race child growing up in Ohio. But Anthony's biggest tests came later in the military, where he spent 22 distinguished and elite years in service to America. His tenacity and grit guided him as he became the first in his family to graduate from college, transition from the enlisted ranks to become an officer, and become incredibly successful in business after his service. His classic rags-to-riches story is a quintessential tale of the American dream.

The common response to his challenges is mental toughness borne out of a deep faith in his gifts and talents and his willingness to go beyond his comfort zone. Even when he failed, rather than fold and resign himself to something less, Anthony redoubled his determination, often capitalizing on his athletic prowess and competitive nature. He parlayed those talents into success in many other areas of his life. He did not compromise and kept his standards high—much in the same vein I wrote about in my book, *The Standard*—and created a purposeful path to his best life.

If you are just starting out, don't feel like you've achieved your dreams, or you're stuck on how to get there, *R.A.C.E. for Greatness* is a godsend for you.

This book is a call to action to find new, compelling, and highly meaningful ways to test your limits. In these pages, you will find detailed road maps to guide you as you work toward your personal vision of success. You'll learn how to find peace among pain, overcome fear, and with a warrior mentality, do the work to elevate your being to places you never thought possible.

R.A.C.E. for Greatness is more than just inspirational platitudes. It is filled with detailed examples and practical steps you can take to turn your aspirations into motivation and, from there, your new reality.

I am honored to lend my voice and support to my friend Anthony for this outstanding book. Read it several times and let the lessons live inside you as you think deeply about how Anthony's wisdom can apply to your life. Then act with force and direction to change your life, just like he did.

The bottom line is this.

Life is a track meet, and it has become more competitive than ever. You need every edge you can use to help you win. *R.A.C.E. for Greatness* is that edge.

In that spirit, with Anthony's help, step up to the starting line and get ready to run and win the most important races of your life.

– Ben Newman, USA Today "Top 5 Mindset & Performance Coaches in the World," 2x Wall Street Journal Bestseller of *The Standard* & *Uncommon Leadership*

Author's Note

As I put the finishing touches on this book, my goal is clear: to equip you with the insights and tools that will transform your journey. Let's set the record straight—this isn't your average motivational read, nor is it merely a collection of strategies or "good ideas." The world is already filled with voices on social media offering advice without substance. But here, we're taking a different path. I'm committed to guiding you through a practical, tactical, and operational blueprint that will elevate both your personal and professional life to unprecedented heights.

We're diving deep, going beyond just laying out the strategic framework. I'm going to walk you through it step-by-step with real-world examples, showing you not just the "what" but the "how." This book is about action—specific, targeted actions that make a real difference. It's about moving beyond the ordinary, pushing the boundaries of what you thought possible, and making tangible improvements where they truly matter.

Prepare yourself for a journey of **Massive, Determined Action**. This is your moment to step into the elite circle of the 1% to harness the full potential of your life and business. Let's embark on this transformative voyage together, armed with the conviction that success is not just a destination but a thrilling journey of continual growth and achievement. Welcome to the turning point of your life.

Table of Contents

R.A.C.E.

RELENTLESS

ATTACK

CONNECTION

EXECUTION

FOR GREATNESS

Introduction

"To give anything less than your best is to sacrifice the gift."
– Steve Prefontaine

Who is this book for?

It's for YOU, Superstar! Are you somewhere between the ages of 21 and 70? Perfect! But, hey, if you're a spry 71 (or older) and eager to go, I want YOU to hop on this roller coaster too! Buckle up because this book is perfect for the business-minded, the daring dreamers, the longtime company loyalists thinking of a change, the freshly laid-off workers, and every budding entrepreneur in between. Are you aiming for the six/seven-figure plus mark? You're in the right place!

Did you know? A whopping five million new businesses sprouted up in 2022. Thanks, Pandemic, for that silver lining! Working in pajamas became a thing, and our entrepreneurial spirit soared! We've been on an uptrend, with a record-breaking 5.5 million businesses birthed in 2021 alone. That's a massive 53% jump from 2019!

Now, for a tiny splash of cold water: about 20% of these newborn businesses will throw in the towel. Yikes! And by the time we hit the five-year mark, only half will be left standing. These odds have hung around like a gloomy rain cloud since the neon-clad '80s and grunge-loving '90s.

But what if, just what if, you had a playbook, a magical guide to dodge the pitfalls and dance through the rain? Voilà! That's where **R.A.C.E. for Greatness** enters the scene, ready to be your shining beacon in a world of fog. Not only will I shower you with stellar strategies, but I'll also dish out the down-to-earth tactics to rake in that dough! Most books will give you plenty of strategy, which I will do, but how many give you tactical ways to execute and create revenue for your business? This book will give you both. You'll get a tried-and-true way to create a million-dollar company, a business, and a life you never imagined.

So, welcome to your soon-to-be-favorite manual for world domination (or at least business greatness)! Grab a comfortable seat, dive in, and let's race our way to the top!

Why Should You Listen to Me? Who Am I?

I am currently the Founder/CEO of a multimillion-dollar company, one of the Top 300 privately held fastest-growing companies in America, and I started it all with nothing!

I had no support system growing up (other than my mother). We will dive deeper into that later. I served in the military for 22 years; I was indoctrinated into the ways of the military: structure, discipline, and standard operating procedures. They told me what to do, and I did it. The only thing I had when I got out of the military was discipline, determination, grit, and grace from God.

It took me over ten years and 10,000 hours to master what I'd done. I want to cut that time in half or make it faster for everyone. I want you to achieve greatness as fast as humanly possible. This book is for every other person in the world who came from nothing, started with nothing, and had no experience but wanted to do something bigger.

I grew up in a small town in Galion, Ohio. That is where they originally made the big yellow machines you saw driving around the country, moving the earth, creating roads in the 1980s. That factory shut down about midway through my childhood, so the town got smaller, and there was not a lot of industry to keep the town going.

It was a lot of farming and small-town business that made up Galion.

My mother was a stay-at-home mother and is the sweetest, most genuine, and caring person in the world. I know she's the best mom, and everyone says their mother is the best. How do I know she was the best? I didn't realize we were poor until other kids told me; she made my home life growing up the best. I thought I was living the best life every day. I remember back in the '80s, we were on the state's free food program, the Women, Infants, and Children's Program (WIC). We got cheese, beans, milk, and eggs. That's where the joke, government cheese, comes from. All of that was delivered to our doorstep. Back then, they didn't give you debit cards to go to the grocery store and get them like we have now.

Around this time, I recall knowing I differed from other kids (poorer). I was in fourth grade and on the free lunch program. Instead of discreetly passing them, they'd call out students like me in front of the class. The gesture was far from subtle, and my classmates didn't hesitate to point out the differences. This was a defining period where I noticed how different my life was from others.

However, fourth grade also introduced me to my knack for selling, although I didn't recognize it for what it was then. While most kids my age dreamed of Atari and gaming systems, those luxuries felt unreachable for someone like me. Yet, when an opportunity arose to win a gaming system by selling spices, I grabbed it with both hands. My drive and determination led me to out-sell everyone.

Post-fourth grade, I transitioned to a quaint Christian school nestled deep in the countryside. It was intimate, with a total strength of forty students from K to Grade 8. It was here that I discovered my talent for running. My speed surprised even me, given the limited competition around me. However, the revelation came at a Christian camp meeting in Ohio. A five-mile race was on the agenda, and I had the perfect pair of leather Air Jordans. While Air Jordans now screamed luxury, they were a $40 pair back then. Those shoes were a testament to my mom's sacrifice, saving every bit she could to gift them to me.

Sporting my bulky leather shoes, I might've looked out of place, but I was determined to complete those five miles. To everyone's surprise, I finished and clinched first place, surpassing not just the kids but all the participants. A pastor, noticing my potential, approached my mom with a suggestion: enroll me in public school, aiming for an athletic scholarship.

It was a turning point. While my initial years were spent in public school up to fourth grade, I later transitioned to a quaint church-affiliated school for the next four years. But now, high school beckoned. We all know the whirlwind that high school can be. And while I shone in athletics, a distinctive aspect of me remained that set me apart.

Born of Chinese and Caucasian descent, with my mother hailing from German lineage, I stood out in the predominantly white town of Galion. My unique looks often drew attention, not always kind, and the financial differences between my peers and me were palpable. The clothes I wore and the things I owned were distinct from those of the more affluent kids, and they didn't hesitate to point it out. But I navigated these challenges, finding solace and pride in athletics. My prowess in sports compensated for much of the disparity I felt elsewhere.

Growing up, my father was a waiter. It wasn't until my time in the military during my twenties that I discovered his significant gambling issues, which kept him away from home and even landed him in jail. As a kid, I believed his absence was due to work commitments, unaware of his incarceration. My mother painted a picture of him working away, which explained the letters he sent me. It was tough, but we persevered. He remained absent from pivotal moments, like my sports events, even when he returned.

As a teenager, life threw me a curveball. At 16, I discovered mutual affection with girls, leading to the birth of my daughter on my high school graduation day. This meant I didn't attend the ceremony. Dreams of college sports scholarships vanished when I realized military academies didn't accept applicants with dependents. This led me to enlist in the Air Force around the Desert Storm era. While serving, I expanded my family with two more kids.

Despite being in the military, our financial situation was tight in the early nineties. I lived in on-base housing and felt the pull for a brighter future. My passion for athletics still burned within me. Balancing my military duties, I pursued a college degree. I initially attended night classes, then switched to daytime when my shifts changed. I benefited from the Airman's Education and Commissioning Program, enabling me to further my education while receiving full pay. This opened the door to officer training school.

All this while, I juggled various part-time jobs—from pizza delivery to hotel clerk shifts, Best Buy to Golden Corral, all to support my growing family. My military pay just didn't cut it. Amidst all this, I trained rigorously for triathlons, aiming for the

2000 Sydney Olympics. Transitioning from enlisted ranks to an officer was a rare achievement I'm immensely proud of. Not only was I the first in my family to graduate from college, but I also became the first military officer. I became part of a small demographic of people who became officers after being enlisted and graduating college as a teenage father. I have been part of the 1% club for a long time (and didn't even know it). I will show YOU how to become part of the 1% club in this book.

My military journey was filled with milestones: from attending the rigorous pararescue indoctrination course, Special Forces Combat Diver Qualification Course, High Altitude Low Opening (HALO) School, and Survival Evasion Resistance and Escape (SERE) training to serving as an acquisition and foreign military sales officer. My dedication culminated in a prestigious role at the Pentagon, working for and alongside the Joint Chiefs of Staff.

After leaving the military, like many of my peers, I was at a crossroads. While some opted for government contractor roles, I was certain that wasn't for me. So, I embarked on an academic journey to pursue a doctorate in psychology. But school life was a stark contrast to my military routine. The hours felt empty compared to the constant hustle of 14-hour shifts at the Pentagon, mixed with rigorous training.

During one of my conversations about the future with my wife, she mentioned a psychologist's potential earnings (around $80k a year). The figure sounded decent, and I was geared toward specializing in sports psychology. However, a detour into the real estate world during my last semester at school completely changed my trajectory. The success was astounding. My earnings in the initial year eclipsed what I'd imagined from a psychology career. I quickly pivoted, diving headfirst into the real estate domain. I expanded into the finance, banking, and mortgage sectors.

Today, I'm the proud founder of a multimillion-dollar mortgage lending company, ZAP Mortgage, and a two-state real estate firm, another multimillion-dollar venture. We've not only secured a spot in the illustrious *Inc. 5000* list for the past two years, placing within the top three hundred, but we also stand as the leading veteran-owned lender nationwide.

This journey of mine stands as testimony. That's where we're at today. That's how I got to where I'm at to share precisely how I did it and prove to everyone that you'll be able to attain greatness no matter where you come from or your circumstances.

CHAPTER ONE

From Battlefield to Boardroom: Harnessing the Power of Mindset and Mental Toughness

"Success is not final; failure is not fatal. It is the courage to continue that counts." – Winston Churchill

Becoming Mentally Tough

The journey to mental fortitude is not a path walked in comfort; it is traversed through adversity, challenges, and the unyielding belief that life's tribulations are not obstacles but stepping stones. My road to resilience was paved without a foundation or support system during my formative years. This isn't a tale of woe, though, far from it. It's a testament to the steel that hardship can forge within us. Can you recall a moment that tested your mind and thought, "This is strengthening me?"

Growing up, I was the odd one out, a half-Chinese kid in a predominantly white town. Kids can be cruel, and their taunts were the anvil on which my mental toughness was hammered into shape.

It wasn't apparent then, but those childhood trials quietly sculpted the resilience I would rely on in the military, in athletics, and in every facet of life. Have you ever realized the trials you once cursed were blessings in disguise?

Let's dive into the crucible that refined my grit: the combined indoctrination course for Air Force Pararescue and Combat Control. Picture this: training so rigorous that, back in the '90s, it whittled down the numbers to such an elite few that PJs were a rarer breed than even Navy Seals. With an attrition rate soaring above 90%, only the toughest of the tough made it through. Can you imagine the level of tenacity required?

Athleticism was my weapon of choice, and I wielded it with the ferocity of a warrior preparing for battle. The pool became my arena, where many faltered, but I found a meditative state among the chaos of "Drown Proofing." Tethered and tossed into the depths, I learned to find peace in the struggle between water and will. Does the thought of such a challenge send shivers down your spine?

Then came the ultimate test of mental and physical fortitude: Buddy Breathing. The symphony of survival played out underwater, sharing a single snorkel with instructors hell-bent on simulating the harshest conditions. The rules were simple yet brutal: keep your head down, share air, and whatever you do, don't come up for air. This wasn't just a test of skill but a trial by water. How would you fare with your lungs screaming and panic clawing at the edges of your mind?

To prepare for this living hell, we did what seemed unthinkable: we deliberately drowned ourselves to overcome the fear, to make peace with the panic. We'd sink to the bottom of the pool, arms wrapped around metal grates until darkness took us. And after our friends pulled us up and we recovered, we'd do it all over again. The dance with the abyss taught us that the brink of failure was a precipice from which we could return. Have you ever pushed yourself to the edge, only to find that the edge keeps moving back?

By hell week, the numbers dwindled, the weak were weeded out, and only the indomitable remained. Nine battered but unbroken souls emerged, a testament to the relentless pursuit of excellence. It's a stark reminder that the crucible of training was not just to become PJs but to prepare for even more grueling challenges, like the Special Forces Combat diving course at Key West. Can you see yourself among that number, weathering the storm to survive and thrive?

This story, this chapter of my life, is shared not as a self-aggrandizing tale but as a beacon for what is possible. It's a call to arms to embrace the hardships and become intimately acquainted with your limits to push past them. It's about becoming the 1%, not just in skill but in spirit. As you stand at the threshold of your challenges, ask yourself: How will you forget your mental toughness? What's your indoctrination course, and are you ready to meet it head-on? The answers lie not in the echoes of the past but in today's actions. Let's face it together, with the fortitude of the military's elite and the heart of a warrior.

In the grand theater of life, where every challenge is a scene, the spotlight doesn't shine on the stage; it illuminates the mind. That's right, the mind is where the drama unfolds, heroes are made, and the narratives of triumph are scripted. The body? It's merely a character following the mind's lead. Picture yourself diving into the deep blue, your heart thumping, your breaths measured. Here, in the depths, I learned to dance with danger, to befriend the blackness of the abyss, trusting in the silent choreography between me and my teammates.

In the rigorous training of a PJ, during the strain of competition, and now in the cutthroat world of business, I chant a mantra that's as rhythmic as it is relentless: "It's gonna suck, it's gonna end." It's a simple truth that applies to everything but the grand finale we all face—death. Each pulse-pounding experience, each gasp-inducing moment, isn't just another day; it's what stitches the fabric of a life well-lived.

Now, imagine strapping on the armor of endurance to tackle seventeen full Ironman triathlons. Think about it: a 2.4-mile swim, a 112-mile bike ride, and a marathon to cap it off. In my heyday, clocking in under 10 hours, I wasn't just taking part; I was soaring through the ranks, becoming part of the elite 1%. Speed was my steed, and I rode it with ferocity.

But let's flip the script from athleticism to pure work ethic. Imagine grinding through a 12 to 14-hour workday and finding the reserves to push the physical envelope. On Saturday, while others rest, I'd launch into a half marathon at 7:00 A.M., chase it with a 60-

mile bike ride at a 21-mph clip, and then, as the sun dipped low, lace up for another half marathon, each step faster than the last. Can you feel the power of the mind orchestrating this symphony of sweat and resolve?

It's a heady concoction, 80% mental and 20% physical. Post-cycling, as my muscles begged for a reprieve, my mind dressed for the second act—an evening run, a race against my morning shadow. No crowds, no applause, just a solitary figure fueled by an internal fire. And Sundays? There was no day of rest but a day of relentless pursuit of two wheels.

Why such a relentless pursuit, you ask? Because for me, it's not about just showing up; it's about seizing glory, being great, and winning. Participation medals don't have a place on my mantle. I chased the thrill of victory, the euphoria of being number one. And if I could marshal my mind to command my body to such feats, so can you. Whatever your arena, be it business, art, or sport—with the right mindset—the finish line is not just a destination; it's your destiny.

So, are you poised to dive into your exhilarating challenge? Are you ready to fan the flames of passion and purpose within your soul? Visualize your triumph, hear the cheers, and feel the weight of the trophy in your hands.

Picture the younger you stepping onto the track, the air electric with anticipation, the stopwatch ready. You're about to shatter records, to redefine possible. Can you see it? Can you believe it?

Now, let's go out there and make it happen. Let your mind lead, your body follows, and the world watches in awe. Ready, set, let's race to GREATNESS!

Mental Toughness of the Military Elite

Under the relentless blaze of the Key West sun, the clear waters beckon with deceptive calm. A battle lies beneath that serene surface, the Army Special Forces Combat Diver Qualification Course (SFCDQC). This isn't just another training program; it's the apex of mental and physical fortitude. Here, Army Special Forces and Navy Seals instructors, with their unwavering gazes, stand as sentinels of discipline, reminiscent of their SEAL counterparts who confront the icy clutches of the Pacific. Salute to those West Coast warriors enduring the frigid embrace of the ocean.

Fueled by the drive to triumph in what's touted as the military's most formidable school, I recall the flashbacks of the grueling indoctrination course. Each memory, each drop of sweat, and every gasp of air serves as a visceral reminder: This is the real deal. It's the infamous "pool week," the proverbial battlefield where dreams take flight or sink into the abyss. Here, failure isn't an option; it's a cliff edge marking the journey's end.

Imagine the ultimate test that fails even the staunchest of hearts—the dreaded "One Man Comp." Envision the water's surface, a mirror to a world above that fades into irrelevance as you submerge. Strapped to your back are twin 80 oxygen tanks, your lifelines in this submerged crusade. The challenge? A mask blackened out, transforming your world into a void where sight is a luxury forfeited. With every controlled breath, the pulse in your temples beats a countdown to the start.

Your lifeline is ripped away, and tranquility turns into a maelstrom. Fingers scramble in darkness, seeking order in chaos. The instructors are not just observers; they're saboteurs, entwining your gear in a Gordian knot of confusion. Your mission amidst their relentless meddling? Stay composed, rectify the chaos, and keep the precious air flowing. This is no mere dive; it's a trial by water, an exercise in composure under pressure. Slip, falter, and the coveted title of Combat Diver could slip away into the depths.

Amidst the turmoil, the "whammy knot," the unsolvable puzzle, emerges. Disorientation seeks to cloud judgment, and a mental battle ensues, pitting instinct against training. One wrong decision, one premature ascent for air, and it's over. But the mantra "Slow is smooth, smooth is fast" pulsates through the mind, a lifeline in disarray.

The challenge doesn't relent with mastery of the undoable knots or knowing your progressions; the instructors, those cunning maestros of psychological chess, ensure the test is relentless. As your lungs clamor for oxygen, the clock stretches out, mocking. Yet, the unbreakable resolve endures and surfaces triumphantly, realizing that victory is not about speed but an unwavering spirit.

When questioned why I remained submerged for four minutes afterward, despite knowing the futility of the "whammy knot," my unyielding determination shines through. It's a refusal to accept anything but the pinnacle of achievement. This is proof that true might isn't measured in muscle, but in the indomitable will that refuses to yield.

So now, are you ready to plunge into such a challenge? Can you muster the courage to discover your aspirations and emerge both successful and extraordinary? The world of GREATNESS awaits, where the realm of champions isn't a distant dream but a reality for those bold enough to chase it. Dive deep into your ambitions, disrupt the stillness, and show the world the champion you are. Are you ready to make some waves? Let's dive into greatness together!

The Course

In the vibrant theater of Key West, where the Atlantic kisses the Gulf of Mexico, the stage is set for a saga of endurance and mastery. The sun is a relentless spotlight, and the ocean is a vast audience awaiting a performance of fortitude. There, the Army SFCDQC beckons—a siren call to the brave and the bold. It's here that I stood, shoulder to shoulder with tenacity, ready to etch my name in the annals of the Department of Defense's most arduous training.

Envision the scene: A rustic manual dive board becomes your underwater chariot, a humble compass atop your guiding star. The ocean, a fluid labyrinth, challenges you to navigate its secrets and safely return to base. Emerge with a score of zero, and you're a navigator extraordinaire; deviate, and the digits tally your misadventure. Can you feel the weight of the ocean's gaze, measuring your every move?

Now, picture the shock, the awe—the sheer incredulity—when, lured by the siren dance of marine life, my dive partner and I surface, not to the reassuring sight of our base but to the colorful streets of Key West. Our detour was so grand our instructors couldn't help but chuckle at our aquatic escapade. Have you ever been so off course that your journey becomes a legend?

With dusk as our backdrop, laden with twin eighty tanks, all our gear, full battle dress uniform, and a faux M16, the ultimatum is delivered: Fail the dive or embark on an odyssey back to base, gear in tow, as the promise of dinner fades with the setting sun. What would you choose? Fueled by hunger, not for food but for triumph, we embarked on a march that tested every fiber of our being. For hours, we trudged, with determination as our compass and the distant barracks as our North Star.

The odyssey continued as we delved into the world of rebreathers—silent sentinels of the deep, leaving no trace of our passage yet fraught with danger. Picture the intensity, the razor's edge of risk and reward. One of my teammates had a caustic cocktail while diving, and the mixture had run down to his genitals and gave him chemical burns in sensitive areas. Did he quit? No, he pressed on the rest of the course because you only get one chance and wasn't giving up. He is a hard *MF'er*! Have you ever pushed through pain, knowing the reward outweighs the agony?

Night descended on us during our last dive, shrouding everything in an inky blanket. The thrill of diving with a rebreather—silent, efficient, leaving no bubble trails—was marred by a sudden, excruciating pain. The searing touch of a Man of War tentacle wrapped around my neck, threatening to derail everything I had worked for. But quitting was not an option.

And I pressed forward just as my friend had previously soldiered on despite the burning chemical mix scalding him. The message was clear—obstacles would arise, and pain would be felt, but giving in was never an option. Emerging victorious, the mark of the tentacle apparent on my swollen face and neck, my instructors commented on my unwavering determination, albeit with a hint of amusement. Slammed some Benadryl in my ass and sent me off to Dreamland. I awoke the next day on the precipice of graduation.

Through these trials, the same resolve that propelled me through the ocean's depths drove my dedication to succeed against all odds. Life, much like the ocean, is unpredictable and capricious. But with a steadfast heart and an unyielding mind, any tide can be turned, any storm weathered.

I invite you to take this journey with me as a tale of underwater misadventures and a testament to the indomitable human spirit. Let it remind you that your mindset, self-definition, and determination can propel you to unimaginable heights. Embrace every challenge, for each is a stepping stone to greatness. Remember, while talent is a gift, effort and grit can bridge any gap. Let's outwork, outthink, and outlast every challenge together.

The Iron Will of Business: A Sport of Mental Fortitude

Close your eyes for a moment, yes, close them, and teleport yourself back to 2013. You're standing at the starting line of Ironman Lake Tahoe, an event that's promised to be nothing short of epic, an electric debut in the annals of Ironman races—the alpine waters of Lake Tahoe stretch before you, embraced by the stoic mountains. Feel the palpable buzz of anticipation from the 2,650 competitors, each a coiled spring of determination and dreams.

Rewind a few days, and the skies were clear, the mood light. But as race day dawned, Mother Nature dealt a wildcard: a whimsical and wild snowfall, blanketing the earth in 3 to 6 inches of white. Imagine waking up when the night still clings to the sky, at 2 or 3 a.m., to a world transformed into a wintry wonderland. The cold bites at your skin, the snowflakes kiss your face, and the dark waters of the lake call out—a challenge, a dare. Your feet tread across the snow, a march of needles against your soles, and the water? It's a paradoxical haven of warmth in the icy air.

But here comes the kicker: despite their meticulous physical prep, a staggering 35% dropped out when the unexpected hit before they even started or failed to reach the finish. They had the muscle, but they didn't have the mindset. When the landscape shifted, did they adapt, or did they retreat? They retreated.

Let's shift the scene to the corporate world, a different endurance test. The stakes? High. The competition? Fierce. The environment is unpredictable. Here, it's not about the diplomas on the wall—it's about the resolve in your heart and the grit in your spirit. Can you see yourself steering through the tumult of market swings and rivalries, undeterred?

Consider this: lenders nationwide might roll out the red carpet for anyone with a license. But is that all it takes? At Zap Mortgage, my flagship company, and within all my ventures, the mental armor counts, not just your credentials (we don't take just anyone). Quality trumps quantity—every single time. This philosophy isn't a page from a new playbook; it's a chapter from the core of my business doctrine, as confirmed in real estate and lending.

We operate with standards etched in stone and displayed for all to see, with no secrets or surprises. During our interviews, it's these standards that candidates must rise to meet, not just the mere possession of a license. And if someone can't keep up, can't hit the high notes we demand? Decisions are made swiftly and surely. Now, ask yourself, what standards do you uphold? Are they etched in stone, immovable in the face of adversity?

Here's the challenge I lay before you: Whether you're an athlete on the cusp of a race or an entrepreneur eyeing the summit of industry, it's time to temper your mind. When the gales howl and the ground shake, will you stand firm or fold?

Business is more than a mere pursuit; it's a sport, a game, and the endgame is victory. It doesn't pause for fatigue or foul weather or yield to excuses. So, set your standards high, rise to the challenge, and let your mental fortitude chart the course to success. Talk is cheap; action is priceless. Don't just dream of greatness; embody it. Are you ready to go beyond words and live out the excellence you aspire to? Let's get to it and conquer the game!

> **Pro Tip:** Visualize the outcome you want daily. Write what you'll do in vivid detail with a date and time in mind. Write it out every day and picture yourself attaining the outcome.

Become the 1%

Imagine this: you're sprinting through the modern business marathon, a landscape that's as cutthroat as it is exhilarating. Every day, you're surrounded by an army of ambitious muscles metaphorically flexed, ready to conquer the world with a battle cry and a PowerPoint presentation. But then, the first hill rises, a challenge appears, and suddenly, the ranks thin. Where did all the warriors go? They've retreated, their mental armor not forged for the actual fight. This is the realm where the infamous 'snowflakes' melt away, revealing the fortitude or lack thereof beneath.

Now, let's talk about an exclusive club, so select it. You might as well have a velvet rope and a bouncer at the door: the illustrious 1% Club. To some, the '1%' whispers tales of ivory towers and gilded hallways. But in our world, our universe of relentless ambition, it's a badge of honor, an emblem of the empire-builders among us.

You've heard of the Pareto Principle, that old 80/20 rule, a concept as vintage as a fine wine, stating that 20% of the people do 80% of the work. But let's shatter that notion with the hammer of reality. After over a decade in the business trenches, I'm calling it— the actual movers and shakers, the real needle-pushers? They're not 20%; they're an elite 1%.

Imagine a workforce, a battalion of potential, but it's the 1% who are the generals, the ones storming the front, catapulting your company into the stratosphere of success. They're the rare breed: the high school footballers who punch their ticket to the NFL, the entrepreneurs who laugh in the face of tax brackets because they're playing in a league far above the million-dollar line.

This pinnacle we speak of, this business Olympus, is not crowded with a top 20%. It's an exclusive summit meeting for the 1%. In my world and in my organizations, it's this 1% who are the titans of industry, hoisting 80% of our revenue on their capable shoulders. And the skeptics, the cynics who cry foul, who say these titans sacrifice joy at the altar of success? They've got it all wrong. These critics are on the outside looking in, not understanding that our 1% aren't just winning at work—they're winning at life.

The champions of the 1% Club aren't vegetating in front of screens or losing themselves in the endless scroll. They're the disciplined, the driven, the dreamers who dare to do. Their world is one where family, business, sports, and more are not just areas of interest—they're fields of conquest.

And let's be clear: the road to this realm is not paved with mere positive thoughts. Vision boards and affirmations? They're the appetizers, not the main course. The feast is action, resilience, and a relentless chase for excellence. It's what separates the 1% from the rest.

Don't be fooled—manifestation alone is a desert mirage. It's the sweat, the grind, the tireless pursuit that turns the mirage into an oasis. You can visualize success every waking hour, but if your reality is saturated with endless Netflix binges and lackluster effort, your dreams will remain just that—dreams. The elite, the true success stories, they're the ones who breathe their aspirations into existence with every action, every decision, every waking moment. Their dedication, perseverance, and unwavering focus carve the path to their aspirations.

So, what about you? Are you ready to lace up your boots to join the ranks of the 1%? Are you prepared to transform your vision into a vivid reality? Let's transcend the ordinary, forgo the path well-trodden, and carve out a highway to the extraordinary. In the game of life, why play to take part when you can play to win? Let's not just talk about success—let's be about it.

Turn the page with me; let's step into the next chapter, a narrative brimming with possibilities and promise. Here, we demystify the enigma of the 1%—that elite cadre of individuals who scale heights and shatter ceilings. They're not just gifted or lucky; they are the indomitable, the steadfast, the relentless. Imagine them not merely as people with innate talent or fortunate stars, but warriors clad in the armor of resolve, wielding the sword of discipline, and bearing the shield of perseverance. They forgo the fleeting allure of instant pleasure for the enduring splendor of monumental achievement.

This is where the race framework comes into play, a potent concoction distilled from the essence of these champions. It's more than a strategy; it's a philosophy, an ethos, a way of life that propels you into the realm of the extraordinary. This book isn't just a read; it's a journey, an odyssey that equips you with the arsenal to break into the hallowed 1% and ascend its ranks to stand tall as a leader among leaders.

Now, as you stand on the precipice of transformation, poised on the brink of your evolution, a question hangs in the balance: Are you ready to embrace the challenge? To ignite the latent greatness that lies within you? To forge not just a path to success, but a legacy of impact?

The journey ahead is not for the faint-hearted. It beckons to those with the audacity to dream and the courage to pursue those dreams relentlessly. It calls to those ready to cast aside the ordinary, eschew the commonplace, and embrace the extraordinary.

So, take a deep breath, steel your resolve, and fix your gaze on the horizon of your highest aspirations. The race is about to begin, and the finish line is nothing less than greatness itself. Are you ready to run this race? To secure your position among the elite? Let's embark on this quest together and unleash the full extent of your greatness.

Key Takeaways

1. **Embrace Adversity as a Catalyst for Growth**: Life's challenges are not meant to be obstacles that halt your progress but rather stepping stones that prepare you for greater achievements. Every trial you face is an opportunity to build resilience. Approach every difficulty with the mindset that it is shaping you into a stronger, more capable individual.

2. **Cultivate Mental Toughness through Real Challenges**: True mental fortitude is forged in the crucible of real-life struggles and rigorous training, not theoretical exercises. Seek out and endure challenges that push your limits, knowing they prepare you for future successes.

3. **Action and Perseverance Are Key to Success**: Success is less about natural talent or luck and more about the willingness to act and persist against all odds. Overcoming setbacks underscores the importance of dogged perseverance and the relentless pursuit of excellence, regardless of the field you're in.

4. **Visualize Success and Set Concrete Goals**: It's gonna suck, it's gonna end; remind yourself that difficult moments will pass and focus on the end goal. Visualization and goal-setting are powerful tools that can help you navigate through tough times by keeping your eyes on the prize and maintaining a forward-moving mentality.

5. **Join the 1% through Discipline and Effort**: Ascending to the top 1% in any endeavor requires an exceptional level of discipline, effort, and a mindset that refuses to settle for mediocrity. Whether in business, sports, or personal development, cultivate the qualities of the elite—unwavering focus, relentless work ethic, and a commitment to excellence. This path is not for everyone, but for those who are willing to put in the work, the rewards are unparalleled.

CHAPTER TWO

R.A.C.E. to Mastery:
Unlocking Tactical Systems for
Breakthrough Success!

"Dream lofty dreams, and as you dream, so shall you become. Your vision is the promise of what you shall one day be. Your ideal is the prophecy of what you shall at last unveil." – James Allen

The Beginning of the R.A.C.E.

Trace the contours of this journey with me, back to where it all began—a time and place where every stride was a sprint against the odds. In the echoing chambers of my past, the term "rat race" resonates not as a cliché but as a palpable reality, a reflection of my footsteps. From these echoes, I derived the acronym R.A.C.E. (Relentless, Attack, Connection, Execution), a compass that has guided me through life's labyrinth toward success and triumph for over half a century.

Now, cast your mind back to the spirited days of the 1980s, to an elementary school where the track was my domain, and competition was my calling. Picture the enthusiasm of a young boy, eyes alight with the blaze of rivalry, heart beating to the drum of foot races. The one hundred meters, the two hundred meters, even the good old sack race—each was a battle, a quest for the blue ribbon. That emblem of victory was more than fabric; it was a flag that marked the conquest of youthful ambition. Can you feel the pulse of anticipation, the taste of triumph on the tip of your tongue?

In those times, there were no consolation prizes, no gentle pats on the back for simply showing up. You stood on the podium, or you watched from the sidelines. The blue ribbon was the champion's garland, the red and yellow mere markers of "almost but not quite." It was a clear-cut lesson—there are winners, and then there are spectators. Do you remember the first time you tasted victory or the sting of being just a hair's breadth away from it?

But let's venture beyond the track to the frostbitten streets of Ohio, where I traded the warmth of home for the thrill of the sale— the prize. A gaming console that heralded the era of digital entertainment. Though she never bore the title, my mother became my sales coach, strategist, and the guiding force behind each knock on a stranger's door. We armed ourselves with scripts, not as a shield against the cold, but as a spear to pierce through the armor of indifference and win that coveted Atari or Odyssey 2. Can you see a young entrepreneur in the making, breath clouding in the frigid air, eyes alight with the fire of ambition?

Poverty was my canvas, and determination my paintbrush. Each spice rack sold was a stroke of color, a blend of persistence and life lessons a mother's wisdom imparted. Can you feel the weight of each sale, not in coins, but in the currency of resilience?

From these experiences, the R.A.C.E. framework was born: *Relentless, Attack, Connection, Execution*. It's a battle cry for the undaunted, a strategy for the bold. As we turn the pages of this book, I won't just narrate the ethos; I'll arm and transform you with it. It's time to transcend inspiration and step into the arena of action.

So, as we embark on this voyage together, I ask you: Are you ready to harness the relentless spirit of the R.A.C.E. framework? Are you prepared to rise from the ranks of the many to the echelons of the few? Join me, and let's unleash the full force of your potential. The race is on—are you ready to run?

It All Starts With One Sale

Picture this: Fresh out of the military, after dedicating twenty-two rigorous years of my life to a world where everything was orchestrated, down to the minute I could take a bathroom break, I stepped into the civilian realm with a hunger I didn't know I possessed. Imagine serving for over two decades in an environment where, for every movement, someone dictates every action else. Now, suddenly, you're free. But what do you do with that freedom?

Enter the realm of real estate. My entire industry knowledge was limited to episodes of *Property Brothers* on HGTV. I was in Denver, far from family, equipped with only a cat (PAWS), an apartment, and a YouTube crash course on selling homes. But I had the fire, the spark, and the resourcefulness. Tony Robbins explains, "It's never a lack of resources, but a lack of resourcefulness."

With just $1,500 in my pocket, bills looming large, and the challenge of establishing myself in a new city, I did what any relentless soul would do. I paced the ritzy streets of Cherry Creek, introducing myself to strangers and asking if they needed a home. The responses varied from alarmed glances to outright hostility, but perseverance pays off. A chance encounter led to my first sale, and suddenly, I wasn't just the rookie anymore. I was Anthony, the real estate agent who got things done.

Fueling this journey was an outlandish goal I set for myself—earning $728,000 in my first year (I just randomly chose a number). I framed this number and placed it prominently on my desk, letting it serve as a daily reminder of the pinnacle I aspired to reach. The end of that year saw me surpassing that target by raking in $748,000. This was my "big why" at that moment, and I looked at it every day; it drove me to be relentlessly obsessed. Every subsequent year? A cool million.

What was the underlying force propelling me forward?—being relentless. It wasn't about having an intricate strategy. It was about diving headfirst with no Plan B, channeling that military discipline, and pursuing my dreams with unyielding vigor. This was the birth of the R.A.C.E. framework, starting with the core principle—**RELENTLESS** pursuit. Are you ready to embrace the **RELENTLESS** drive within you?

Dive deep into the profound significance of the letter "R" in the acronym R.A.C.E. It stands for **RELENTLESS**, but this isn't just an ordinary word. It's a war cry, a battle stance, and a mantra all wrapped. Picture this: an indomitable spirit that thrives on challenges to overcome and obliterate them. Do you have that fire? The fire that keeps burning no matter how torrential the rain is?

In my narrative, my life became a manifestation of relentless ambition and undeniable proof that when I say I'll do something, I do it with obsession, with an intensity that often leaves those around me feeling a mix of awe and unease. Tell me, when you voice your aspirations, do people squirm? Do they question? Because if they don't, perhaps your dreams aren't lofty or daring enough.

Rewind to my early days in real estate. Picture Cherry Creek: a pristine heartland of million-dollar properties with seasoned agents who'd been in the game for decades. These stalwarts had seen and heard it all except me. Here I was, green, inexperienced, but with a spark and a sales starter kit I'd acquired for $97. That course was like my Bible, filled with rudiments like letter writing and referrals.

And then there was my audacious goal: $728,000. I displayed it proudly, defiantly, on my desk. I wanted everyone to see, to know. But instead of rallying cheers, I mostly received stifled chuckles and patronizing smirks. Imagine walking into a realm with the notion that everyone's part of a larger team, a united front. But the reality? Far from it. Instead of collaborative mornings and shared targets, my proposal for team efforts was met with echoing silences. Day in and day out, I'd be the lone soldier, preparing my materials and getting ready to conquer. While others sneered or ignored me, I embraced the power of consistency.

But the universe has a funny way of turning tables. Fast forward seven months, and guess who was standing at the pinnacle? The once ridiculed rookie was now the *numero uno* broker in the office, outclassing agents with two decades of experience. Those skeptics were now queuing up, eager to collaborate on the properties I was handling. Why? Because I was unyielding, unwavering, relentless.

But there's more to the story. Next came the imperative to **ATTACK**—the "A." And no, I'm not talking about conceptualizing strategies over a cup of coffee or plastering motivational quotes on social media. Attack means diving into the trenches, taking formidable, purposeful steps daily, tackling every challenge head-on, and driving toward your vision. It's about identifying the problem and actively seeking and implementing solutions.

So, let me challenge you: are you ready to be **RELENTLESS**? Are you geared up to **ATTACK** your dreams? Dive in, for the journey has just begun.

When in Doubt—ATTACK

Imagine a picturesque summer day in the mountains of eastern Virginia, the site of a local but extremely competitive triathlon (like the Super Bowl of triathlons in Virginia). Let's set the record straight. This wasn't the grueling Ironman. This was an Olympic distance triathlon, which might sound simpler to the uninitiated, but it poses its unique challenges. One is expected to swim a mile, bike for twenty-four miles, and then run a 10k.

Now, picture the glistening morning sun, the scent of competition in the air, and the collective thud of excited hearts, mine included. The swim was to be my first conquest. But alas! The water was not my friend that day. I was trailing, overtaken by seasoned swimmers and even agile 12-year-olds. And while it's true that there are some exceptionally quick 12-year-olds out there, I want you to grasp the gravity of my position: I emerged not with the leading pack but lagging in the back.

Imagine the range of emotions that surged within me. Frustration? Absolutely. Despair? Momentarily. But the spirit of a fighter? Eternally! I had choices at that crucial juncture, the crossroads of resolve and resignation. I could have surrendered to mediocrity, merely floated through the motions, or even worse, considered the taboo word quit. But winners don't think of the finish line; they think of the journey. And I decided to **ATTACK**!

During my intensive triathlon training phase, my trusty heart rate monitor had been a constant companion. It dictated my rhythm, guiding me to maintain specific speeds and exertions. My goal? To optimize my performance using detailed metrics, I ensured my heart rate was aligned with the power I was pushing out on the bike. Yet, given the odds against me after that lackluster swim, metrics suddenly seemed too restricting. So, in a split-second decision, a metaphorical shedding of old beliefs, I discarded my heart rate monitor. Can you feel that thrill? That heady rush of abandoning the familiar and diving headlong into the unknown?

Now unleashed, I mounted my bike and pedaled with a ferocity I hadn't known before. My mind was free from numerical constraints, and all I could focus on was reclaiming lost ground, one rapid, powerful pedal stroke at a time. With no digital numbers to preoccupy me, I trusted my instincts and body. After an intense biking spree, with my legs burning and lungs heaving, I transitioned into the run. Shoes laced, I charged forth, never glancing at a watch or seeking validation from a device.

Flash forward to the last stretch—just half a mile to go. I recalled days when I could clock under two minutes for this distance. And as if on cue, my legs tapped into a hidden reservoir of energy. Ahead, the leader's silhouette came into view. I closed the gap with each stride until I was not just beside him but blazing past. The transformation was miraculous, from trailing at the back during the swim to clinching victory.

But what's the real takeaway? Sometimes, our greatest adversaries aren't others but our self-imposed limitations. For me, that day, it was the heart rate monitor, a symbol of my self-imposed barriers. By casting it aside, I attacked the race and my apprehensions. So, I challenge you: What's holding you back? What's your "heart rate monitor"? Recognize, discard, and charge forward; life waits for no one. Always be on the **ATTACK**!

It Takes a Village

Deepen your breath and allow me to take you on an intricate journey through the intricate tapestry of connections that shape and define our lives. As we weave our path through the world, one essential element forms the lifeblood of our endeavors: **CONNECTION** (the "C"). Whether it's an invisible thread or a sturdy rope, the connections we cultivate determine the richness of our experiences and the narrative of our success.

Reflect on this: Imagine a vast, intricate web, where every strand represents a connection—some thin and delicate, others thick and sturdy. As part of this immense tapestry, you must be intertwined with various aspects of your life: yourself, your spouse, your family, your clients, and even your business associates. It's not just a pleasant aspect; it's the keystone of any worthwhile endeavor.

Drawing from my rich tapestry of experiences, from the disciplined corridors of the military to the dynamic business world, I've come to appreciate the art of connection. With its rigid hierarchies and formidable reputations, the military is not an obvious playground for building connections. Yet, despite my junior enlisted rank, my connections with senior officers catapulted me ahead when I set my sights on getting into the Airman's education and commissioning program. Their letters of recommendation weren't mere formalities but testaments to the relationships I had cultivated, even within such a structured environment.

Then there was the Pentagon, an institution famed for its bureaucratic mazes. Understanding the playbook wasn't enough to navigate its complex corridors and even more intricate hierarchies. Real success hinged on building relationships and forging connections, transcending rank and file.

In athletics, where sheer talent and determination are celebrated, you might think connections are secondary. Yet, even here, whether securing sponsors for those perfect-fit shoes or ensuring I had a spot in the most coveted races, my ability to genuinely connect with others made the difference.

But allow me a moment to shift gears to the bustling business realm. Beyond the spreadsheets, marketing campaigns, and profit margins lies the heart of any successful venture: relationships/connections. Clients, colleagues, employees—it isn't merely about transactions; it's about forging bonds that stand the test of time. Remember this: "Relationships over transactions." Inscribe it in your heart and mind. Because in a world increasingly driven by instant gratifications and one-off deals, building and nurturing relationships ensures a legacy of continued transactions.

In my academic pursuits, while penning a paper for my MBA, I delved into "Transformational vs. Transactional Leadership." But this dichotomy extends beyond the boardroom—it's a philosophy for life. Being transformational means looking beyond the immediate, fostering growth, and inspiring change. Meanwhile, being merely transactional is short-lived, often lacking depth.

Embrace transformation. Become a servant leader, one who prioritizes the growth and well-being of others over personal gain; the best example of this is Jesus Christ, for it's in this metamorphosis, this shift from transactional to transformational, that genuine success—both in business and in life—blooms. Challenge yourself: In which areas of your life can you be more transformational? How can you prioritize deep, meaningful connections over fleeting interactions? Dive deep into this introspection, and you'll discover a wellspring of potential waiting to be unleashed.

Want the Keys to the Castle?—Execution

Let's jump in headfirst and take an exhilarating ride through the world of execution, where dreams are made real, and actions speak louder than words. Let me paint a vivid tapestry of what it means to execute genuinely and dare you to rise to the challenge.

As we reach the pinnacle of our equation, we arrive at the letter "E," representing **EXECUTION.** This pivotal component is where most dreams falter, and ideas crumble. Think about it; you might possess the vision, passion, and even the best-laid plans, but without **EXECUTION,** it's all just smoke and mirrors. Here's where the rubber meets the road; only the committed will thrive.

Let's step into a time capsule and rewind to 1994. Picture me, an energetic 21-year-old, soaking in my squadron's break area camaraderie. Another eager airman, full of youthful zeal, approached, unveiling what he believed was his ticket out—a business idea. He mapped out his envisioned empire with each slide of his painstakingly created PowerPoint and meticulously detailed Excel sheets. I cheered him on, genuinely hopeful for his venture. But here's the twist: merely three months later, instead of launching his dream, he reenlisted in the military. His beautifully crafted plans? They remained just that—plans. He had everything but the crucial "E": **EXECUTION**.

Now, let's jump forward to some of the most electrifying conferences I've attended, Unleash the Power Within, with renowned motivational speakers like Tony Robbins at the helm. Imagine the palpable energy, the fervor, and the waves of inspiration crashing over attendees. I've connected with many of these impassioned souls and watched as some formed groups, endlessly discussing their ambitions. But here's the catch: While many continue to chase that high level of motivation, only a few, less than 1%, genuinely heed Tony's call and spring into action. Many bask in the euphoria, swept up in grand visions and lofty words, only to let inertia set in soon after.

Execution isn't about sporadic bursts of enthusiasm; it's about unwavering commitment. It's the heartbeat of relentless pursuit, of taking massive, deliberate steps toward your dreams and never letting go, no matter what happens.

Imagine the R.A.C.E. Performance system as an intricate, high-performance engine, with every cog and wheel in impeccable harmony. It's a marvel of precision, where the sum of all parts works in concert to produce a surge of forward momentum. This isn't about understanding each component in isolation but choreographing them into a symphony of efficiency that elevates your capabilities to new heights.

Picture yourself as this engine's driver, the symphony's maestro. Each piece of the system is an instrument awaiting your command, ready to play its part in the grand performance of your pursuit. But how will you direct this orchestra of potential? Can you feel the thrill of synchronizing these elements, not just for mere performance, but for the mastery that leads to greatness?

As we prepare to delve into the intricacies of this system, I throw down a thrilling challenge that could set your pulse racing. Are you equipped to embark on this sprint toward greatness, not just mentally, but in the very fiber of your being? This isn't a leisurely jog in the park; this is the sprinter's dash—fierce, unrelenting, and blistering.

Are you part of that elite cadre who transform daydreams into dynamic action? The starting pistol has sounded, and the track lies ahead. Are you ready to take the leap and land among the stars of **EXECUTION**? The challenge is cast before you in all its thrilling glory. Your next move is a testament to your readiness. Will you step up? The race for greatness is on, and your place at the starting line awaits. Are you ready to take it?

Key Takeaways

1. **Embrace the Relentless Pursuit of Your Goals**: The essence of the R.A.C.E. framework begins with being relentless. It's about having a fierce, unwavering commitment to your dreams and ambitions. Challenge yourself to adopt this relentless spirit in pursuing your own goals, pushing beyond your comfort zone, and never settling for mediocrity.

2. **Attack Your Objectives with Precision and Passion**: Taking action is paramount. The narrative emphasizes the importance of attacking your objectives, not with half-hearted effort but with full commitment and strategic execution. It's the bold steps and the willingness to dive into the trenches that differentiate the successful from the spectators. Ask yourself, how can you apply a more aggressive, focused approach to your aspirations?

3. **Cultivate Deep and Meaningful Connections**: Success is not a solo journey. The strength of your connections—with peers, mentors, clients, and even competitors—can significantly influence your trajectory. You must prioritize building authentic connections that enrich both your personal and professional life. Reflect on how you can foster stronger bonds and a supportive network around you.

4. **Execute with Excellence and Urgency**: Execution is where ideas transform into outcomes. The difference between dreaming and achieving lies in your ability to execute with precision, excellence, and urgency. Challenge yourself to move beyond the planning phase

and into the realm of tangible results. Consider what steps you can take today to move closer to your goals.

5. **Harness the Power of the R.A.C.E. Framework for Mastery**: Finally, the R.A.C.E. framework is presented as a comprehensive strategy for achieving breakthrough success. It's a call to not just aspire to greatness but to actively pursue it through relentless effort, strategic action, meaningful connections, and flawless execution. Reflect on how you can incorporate these principles into your daily life, setting the stage for personal and professional mastery.

Are you ready to rise to the challenge? Will you adopt the relentless spirit, attack your goals with precision, cultivate meaningful connections, execute with excellence, and harness the R.A.C.E. framework to unlock your full potential? The path to mastery awaits, and the race is yours to run.

CHAPTER THREE

Tenacity Unleashed—The Essence of Relentlessness

"Being the best means engineering your life so you never stop until you get what you want. Then you keep going until you get what's next. And then you go for even more."
– Tim Grover, Relentless, 2013

Let's jump with both feet into the realm of unyielding perseverance. By the time we emerge, I hope to challenge you to acknowledge and genuinely embrace **RELENTLESSNESS** in your life's pursuits. So, what does it mean to be genuinely **RELENTLESS**?

Being relentless doesn't just mean pushing past barriers. It means shattering them, transcending them, and defying every single voice that whispers, *Maybe it's time to give up.* It's an unwavering, unbreakable commitment, the sort of passion that says, "I would rather face the harshest of outcomes than accept defeat.

Let's rewind in 2015. Picture the iconic Boston Marathon—a grueling stretch from Hopkinton, Massachusetts, to Boston's heart. Even before the race begins, it's a testament to commitment:

participants brave early wake-up calls, long bus rides, and pre-race nerves. I was one of them. Months of training had me poised to finish in 2 hours 45 minutes, a target I was persistent about.

But here's the twist. Mother Nature had other plans. The forecast was dire: 45 degrees, drenching rain, and blistering 20 mph headwinds. Many people might balk at the thought, even reconsider taking part. But for me? It was just the weather. Whether facing rigorous challenges in the military or braving the diverse conditions in athletics, I've always maintained that the weather is but a backdrop. Our spirit, drive, and commitment? Those are front and center.

As we assembled under tents in Hopkinton, MA (26.2 miles away from Boston), the chilly rain was our constant companion, and anticipation built. When the starting gun finally sounded, the elements were the last thing on my mind. Ten miles in, a sharp pain made an unwelcome appearance. My foot had popped, and by the time I hit the halfway mark, each step felt like a dagger driven into my foot. Yet, here's where relentlessness shines its brightest. Instead of giving in, I adapted. Despite a suspected broken foot, rain, and the cold, surrender was not in my vocabulary.

The marathon became more than just a race. It was a testament to spirit and willpower. My swollen foot and the excruciating pain only amplified my determination. I tightened my laces, mentally braced myself, and hobbled on, each step a declaration of indomitable spirit.

And as I crossed that finish line, the slower-than-anticipated time was eclipsed by the triumph of spirit. My wife's relief was palpable—she'd seen me conquer many a race, but never at this pace. The aftermath? A foot adorned with two screws and a subsequent surgery, thanks to my overzealous approach to recovery.

But the marathon, the pain, and even the surgeries weren't the focal points. It was the lesson they collectively taught. Being relentless is about pushing boundaries, challenging your status quo, and proving to yourself that limits are mere constructs of the mind. So, I challenge you: In the marathon of life, will you merely run, or will you be relentless in your pursuit of the finish line? With each step of this narrative, I challenge you: dare to dream big, aspire to be relentless, and let's journey together!

Shortly after you turned the pages of this book and *R.A.C.E. for Greatness* was on bookshelves, I embarked on an audacious quest— The Grand Slam Marathon Challenge. This isn't just any ordinary running challenge. It's a global journey across six marathons: Tokyo, Boston, London, Berlin, Chicago, and New York City, the largest marathons in the world, known as "The Majors." It sounds like a lifetime achievement, doesn't it? Most people think so, often spanning 6 to 20 years to complete them all.

To bring this into sharper focus, just a minuscule 0.5% of marathoners globally achieve this feat, running them all within a single year. Well, that's uncharted territory. But here's where things get even trickier. If you imagine this task is about stamina and the will to run, think again— it is the challenge of entering these coveted races.

Getting a spot in one of these marathons isn't a simple click-and-register deal like your local 5k. Oh no. It's a dance of endurance long before the race starts. To give you a slice of the challenge, the London Marathon 2023 was inundated with a staggering 550,000 applications, all vying for a mere 30,000 spots.

Gaining entry was an intense marathon—a marathon of persistence. This meant months of relentless outreach, countless rejections, meticulous research, and many "Nos." But with unwavering focus, I earned my place in all six, from historic Boston to the vibrant New York City Marathon. Passion keeps you moving, even when the world says stop. My story is but a prelude to another tale of grit, one I believe will strike a chord with everyone.

A Mother's Relentless Pursuit

Imagine a young mother of two trying to navigate family responsibilities while also seeking to carve out a place for herself in the world. Meika was a beacon of potential, brightening her world as a server at the local steakhouse. Yet, deep within her lay the embers of a dream that was about to ignite.

She embarked on a journey in my company without a college degree and juggling responsibilities. The climb was steep, and the path was fraught with challenges. However, Meika's relentlessness, akin to that of a determined marathoner, kept her pressing forward.

With two young children at her side and armed with sheer determination, she dove headfirst into the mortgage world.

While most would've buckled under pressure month after month, she pressed on, fueled by an insatiable drive to provide a better life for her children. And then the tides turned. Six months in, her income soared, surpassing her previous year's earnings.

In a brief span, she elevated her life and became a beacon of hope for others, specializing in down payment help and government loans. Meika went the extra mile with every client, providing a service that was nothing short of extraordinary.

Beyond her work, she's a devoted mother and wife, and her commitment to self-improvement saw her return to college—all while maintaining her unyielding drive at work. And here's the heartwarming twist: this incredible woman, Meika, is my daughter.

Her journey is a testament to the relentless spirit I've always championed. Raised to witness my relentless pursuits, from triathlons to business, she took those lessons and forged her legacy of perseverance.

And so, dear reader, remember Meika's story and my marathon journey as you delve further into this book. We all have our races to run and our challenges to overcome. It's the relentless spirit, the unwavering commitment, and the insatiable hunger for success that will see us through. Embrace it, nurture it, and let's run our races together!

The Lonely Path of Relentlessness

Here is a powerful thought: if a mother with two young ones, battling time, fatigue, and myriad responsibilities, can chase and capture her dreams, why can't you? What's holding you back? Embrace the challenge! Let's embark on an exhilarating exploration of what it truly means to be relentless in pursuing your dreams. I want you to fasten your seatbelts and get ready because this journey is bound to challenge your convictions, inspire you, and even jolt you out of complacency.

Being relentless often places you on a path that can be, for many stretches, solitary. This is a path where even friends who once cheered for your every move may suddenly fall silent or become detractors.

We humans crave social connections. We're wired to bond with our tribes, our groups of like-minded souls. But a relentless pursuit might throw you a curveball. Many will not comprehend your passion as your drive takes you in new directions. They might dub you "crazy" or "over-ambitious." But here's where your mettle is tested. Do you bend to the naysayers or rise with even more determination?

During my transition from running a successful real estate brokerage to embarking on an even grander venture, many labeled me "insane." Those very lenders I'd collaborated with for years suddenly doubted my capabilities. Their words were biting, steeped in skepticism. But between the lines, I could read their fears—they were threatened by my ambition, worried that my new endeavor would overshadow their businesses.

I wasn't out there to crush anyone's dreams or businesses, but to realize my own. My focus was laser-sharp—on my company's potential, unique path, and destined milestones. Yet, through my journey, I made a point: relentless grit and undying passion make the impossible possible.

The response to my new venture? Of the many lenders I had partnered with over a decade, only two genuinely congratulated and supported me. Just two out of hundreds! But that didn't deter me. Their doubt fueled my fire even more.

The Evolution of Connections

With growth and **RELENTLESS** dedication, there's an inevitable evolution—not just in what you do, but in who you surround yourself with. Friends evolve. You'll find that as your priorities shift, so does your circle. Over the past 12 years, my friend's group has transformed drastically.

For instance, there were the cherished poker nights. Oh, how I loved those games with a close-knit group! But as my dedication grew, late Friday nights followed by early work mornings became unrealistic. Many of my friends understood, even though invites became rare. They supported me in their unique way, understanding that my journey had taken a different turn.

However, remember this: new, like-minded individuals will take their place as some fade from your immediate circle. These individuals resonate with your mission, amplify your passion, and support your relentless journey.

In conclusion, while relentless ambition may come with challenges, the rewards are unparalleled. Embrace the journey, accept the evolution, and always keep your eyes on the prize. Now, ask yourself: Are you ready to be relentless? Let's forge ahead together! Get ready to tap into your limitless potential!

Relentlessness: A Life Philosophy

Have you ever considered the power that relentless focus can bring to each dimension of your life? While every day might seem like a scene from a familiar movie, the cast can change. Let's get this straight: my friends from a decade ago are still my friends. One is gearing up alongside me for the New York City marathon in 2024. Still, as life's tides shift, our focus must evolve.

Can you always be the friend who lounges around, catching every movie premiere or football game? The uncompromising truth? No. Certain sacrifices are essential if you genuinely wish to etch your name in the annals of greatness. This unwavering focus on your goals, sometimes at the expense of leisure, is the core of relentless living.

To quote John Wooden, "You will never outperform your inner circle." Your inner environment is a direct reflection of your outer world. This relentless attitude isn't about worldly achievements but mastering control over the one thing you can do: yourself. In business, health, or family, the relentless pursuit is often intertwined with another gem: discipline.

Think of sporting legends like Kobe Bryant or Michael Jordan. Their daily regimen wasn't about the games; it was about waking up at dawn, even on game days, sweating it out, practicing, refining, and then practicing some more. Kobe's stories aren't just anecdotes; they're a testament to a lifestyle where, in one year, he accomplished more than many could in a lifetime.

The Mathematics of Dedication

Let's get into some fun arithmetic here. Imagine I start my day at 4:00 a.m. By the time you hit the snooze button for the third time, I've wrapped up my workout and powered through many emails. I've effectively gained a five-hour lead if you take until 9:00 a.m. to get where I was at 4:00 a.m. Add a couple of extra evening hours to my relentless daily grind, and the total rises to seven hours. Now, multiply this by the number of days in a year. Mind-blowing. Adjusting my schedule slightly, I've achieved what many can't, even in months.

Take a cue from Arnold Schwarzenegger's playbook: "Just sleep a little faster." The Terminator himself believes in sleeping less and in the magic of six hours of sleep. I resonate with that. The secret isn't in the quantity but in the waking's quality hours—the distinction between the ordinary and the extraordinary lies in this optimized utilization of time.

Control, Focus, and Results

To give you a taste of relentlessness in action: In the past year and a half, while global economic tides turned tumultuous and interest rates skyrocketed, my enterprise didn't just stay afloat; we thrived. It wasn't magic—it was control. No, I can't dictate global interest rates. But I can undoubtedly dictate my response to them.

By consistently controlling our actions and guiding my vibrant, albeit occasionally wild, team of loan officers, we've carved our path to success. Our secret weapons? The R.A.C.E. Million Dollar Business template and daily accountability tracker (I have made free ones for you to download). These tools ensure we're laser-focused and on point with all tasks daily.

****Download the Daily Scorecard and
Million Dollar Template Here****

It's no myth; those who incorporate this relentless discipline into their daily routines are the ones you'll often find enjoying six and seven-figure incomes. This isn't about extravagance; it's about potential realized. When you see relentless focus's tangible benefits in your life, you'll not only adopt it, but you'll also embody it.

I challenge you now to stand up wherever you are. Feel the ground beneath your feet, the air on your skin. Now, visualize all the insights you've gained and the willpower you've mustered to embrace relentlessness. Can you see it? That's the weapon you're armed with, and it's not just any weapon—it's a force of nature, a tidal wave of determination.

Now, imagine the days ahead. Each sunrise presents a battlefield with opportunities, challenges, twists, and turns. But here's the thing: with your relentless spirit, not only can you face these challenges, but you can also conquer them, turning every adversity into a stepping stone.

Dive deep, headfirst into this process! Don't just dip your toes in—submerge yourself. Embrace the challenges like a long-lost friend. Why? Each challenge will only polish your relentless spirit, making it shine brighter, fierce enough to be visible even from the farthest star.

So, here's the ultimate question: Are you prepared to push beyond your known boundaries? Are you prepared mentally and physically to redefine the very essence of your limits? This isn't just any challenge; it's a call to greatness, a summons to your inner warrior. Do you accept this challenge, ready to show the world the true might of your relentless spirit? Will you rise to the occasion?

Now that you are **RELENTLESS**, it is time to learn to **ATTACK**! This is where you take that newfound spirit and put it into motion.

Key Takeaways

1. **Embrace Relentlessness as a Core Value**: Being relentless isn't just about persistence; it's about an unwavering commitment to your goals, breaking through barriers, and never settling for less. It's a mindset that doesn't recognize the word "quit."

Challenge yourself: How can you cultivate this relentless spirit in your own pursuits, pushing beyond your perceived limits?

2. **Adapt and Overcome**: The journey to success is filled with unexpected challenges, as seen in the author's marathon experience and the rigorous process of entering the world's major marathons. Being relentless means adapting to circumstances without losing sight of your goals.

Challenge: Are you willing to adapt and find creative solutions to overcome them?

3. **Draw Inspiration from Those Around You**: The story of Meika, a young mother who transitioned from a server to a successful mortgage specialist, illustrates that relentlessness can lead to extraordinary achievements regardless of your starting point. Let this inspire you to pursue your dreams with tenacity, regardless of your current situation.

Ask yourself: What dreams have you been holding back on, and what first step can you take today?

4. **Understand the Loneliness of the Path**: Pursuing greatness can sometimes mean walking a path less traveled, which can be lonely and misunderstood by others. Recognize that being relentless in your pursuit may distance you from some while aligning you closer with others who share your vision and drive.

Challenge: Are you ready to embrace the solitude that comes with relentless pursuit and find strength in your journey?

5. **Leverage Relentlessness in Every Aspect of Life**: Relentlessness is not just about achieving a single goal; it's a life philosophy that can be applied to personal development, professional growth, and even in building and maintaining relationships. Consider how being relentless can transform your approach to daily tasks, long-term goals, and interactions with others.

Challenge: How can you apply a relentless approach to achieve a balance of success across different facets of your life?

Now, are you ready to take up the challenge? Will you let the essence of relentlessness infuse every part of your life, breaking through barriers, and achieving what you once thought impossible? Remember, the path to greatness is paved with the relentless pursuit of excellence. Let's embark on this journey together, armed with the conviction that there are no limits to what we can achieve when we harness the power of relentlessness.

CHAPTER FOUR

Art of the Attack

"The difference between a successful person and others is not a lack of strength, not a lack of knowledge, but rather a lack in will."
– Vince Lombardi

Prepare for an adventure, a story of sheer tenacity, and a lesson in the art of the **ATTACK**. As you join me on this journey, remember it's not just about hearing another tale—it's about envisioning yourself in these shoes, pushing limits, and reshaping your reality. Are you ready? Let's begin.

Attack from All Sides

Picture the energetic, bustling city of Denver, Colorado. Freshly inked pages of my life's book were waiting to be filled when I landed here, ready to pen a new chapter. My toolbox? Not filled with the usual handyman's favorites, but with a pair of running shoes, an open heart, and a mind wired for forging connections.

I had a simple strategy, but it was anything but easy—I plunged into the community's pulse. Every day, come rain or shine, I was out there, joining a running club, where the mornings were brisk, and the nights were alive with the pounding of determined feet on the pavement. And yes, Sundays, too. You might wonder, what's the big deal about running? But it wasn't about the miles. It was about the people, the shared sweat and laughter, and the community built stride by stride.

But why stop running? With a voracious appetite for connection, I did yoga on the Capitol steps twice weekly. Now, let's be clear: yoga and I were not a match made in heaven. I was as flexible as a two-by-four, but I did it. I did it because I saw potential in every stretch, every pose—an opportunity to meet potential homeowners, the fabric of Denver's future.

The Red Rocks beckoned to workout warriors, and I enthusiastically answered their call. Hiking groups, you ask? I was there, scaling heights with fellow adventurers, each peak becoming a networking summit. And let's not forget about the bike rides. I joined a racing team, and with every push of the pedals, I sprinted toward future business opportunities.

Evenings? They weren't for resting; they were for expanding horizons. Beer clubs at night became my unconventional boardrooms, and business meetups were my battlegrounds for connection. And through it all, I attacked every opportunity with the fervor of a general leading a charge.

You may wonder how I found the time. It's simple. I was in attack mode, the only mode I knew after 22 years in the disciplined world of the military. Sales was a new battleground, but relationships? That was my forte. And so, for two years, for 15 or more hours a day, every single day, I committed myself fully to this cause. I didn't just work; I lived and breathed this mission.

The result? I became a fixture in the Denver scene. Not just another face in the crowd but "the pink tie guy," known for my sartorial flair and relentless networking. It wasn't about asking for business but about being present consistently, authentically, and relentlessly.

Now, let's fast forward to 2021, to a challenge of a different kind—the Coast to Coast (C2C) adventure race across Florida. This was no ordinary race; it was an expedition of over three hundred miles, a test of endurance, navigation, and sheer will. Preparing for it meant juggling a thriving business daily and morphing into an orienteering maestro by night.

When race day dawned, the **ATTACK** strategy came into full swing. I segmented this behemoth of a challenge into bite-sized battles. I gave it my all for each leg of kayaking and each stretch of mountain biking. My competitors became mere blips on my radar, each checkpoint a conquered territory. And through it all, my relentless spirit, the warrior within, roared louder with every mile.

Now for the finale of a race—an arduous journey across the rugged terrain of Florida. As I dashed across the finish line, lungs heaving and muscles screaming, a mix of emotions surged. Yes, I had come in first but missed some checkpoints. I didn't clinch the official win, but in my heart, I knew I had conquered.

Now, let's pause and reflect. When you ponder your own goals, do they make your pulse race? Do they seem like Goliaths in the face of your David? If not, it's time to redraw those lines, to draft dreams so vast they send shivers down your spine. Because, my friend, the goals that scare you and send that delicious tremor of fear mixed with excitement through your veins are worth chasing.

Envisioning and embarking on endeavors like racing across Florida or tackling all six marathon majors in a year is the colossal ambition that gets my blood pumping. That's what I mean by "scared"—a positive, electrifying fear that propels you to leap into action, to relentlessly attack each day as if it's your last chance to make an impact.

Life doesn't come with a rewind button. Every moment you're not, you're standing still. To attack isn't just a physical act; it's a mentality. It's waking up daily with a laser focus on one goal, dismissing distractions like those proverbial squirrels that dart across your path.

I watch with amusement and dismay as the internet's self-proclaimed gurus, who've yet to build anything of substance, dole out advice like candy. They'll tell you to diversify, to spread yourself thin across multiple hustles. But here's the unvarnished truth: they're leading you astray.

Yes, multiple income streams are a financial nirvana, but that comes later. In this chapter of your life, you must pour all your energy into one vessel. Mastery of one thing—that's the key to unlocking doors to the future you desire.

Consider the bucket of water analogy. If you thinly spread that water across ten cups, you'd have a collection of partially filled vessels. But concentrate that water into one cup, focus your efforts, and not only will it be full, but it will also overflow. That's the power of the "one thing" philosophy.

This singular focus allowed me to excel in one area, to create a torrential downpour of success that eventually overflowed, creating streams that flowed into other ventures and other opportunities. It's the power of compounded effort—one focus, one goal, one relentless pursuit.

As I have, you can harness this focus to excel in one domain first. That excellence becomes the wellspring for other ventures, allowing you to cascade gracefully into various income streams.

Settle in, adventurers of ambition, for another chapter in our saga of success and the mastery of the mundane, the grandeur of grit, and the celebration of single-minded focus. Ready your minds and hearts, for this tale is not just a recounting of events—it's a blueprint for the victories you can claim.

Embracing the Mundane

In a world where the mundane is often skirted around, and the routine is dodged like an unpleasant chore, I present a different narrative—one where the mundane is embraced and mastered. Let's turn the spotlight on Lorne, a maestro of the mundane whose journey epitomizes the power of focusing on the basics.

From the cozy confines of my home, where the air buzzes with the potential of sales calls, Lorne embarked on his maiden voyage into the world of live calling. His first attempt? Let's say it was less than stellar. My wife, a seasoned connoisseur of sales pitches, exchanged a glance with me that said volumes. But Lorne? He didn't flinch. Instead, he returned, day after day, each time better than the last, transforming the dull hum of repetitive practice into a rhythm of inevitable success.

The Power of Coaching and Teamwork

Herein lies a precious lesson: the journey to mastery need not be solitary.

"If you want to go fast, go alone. If you want to go far, go together."

This wisdom speaks to the essence of teamwork and coaching. It's a call to arms of those willing to learn, improve, and hold each other up. And it's a testament to the fact that we can achieve more together, and our successes are sweeter, shared among comrades in arms.

Over a career that spanned thousands of sales calls, I can attest to the transformative power of repetition. It's a metamorphosis from mere participant to master communicator, where every day's attack on the task at hand builds an unstoppable momentum. It's about waking up with the fire of a thousand suns, ready to seize the day and turn "boring" into "brilliant."

The 100-Point Daily Success Scorecard

As you'll discover with our R.A.C.E.'s 100-point daily success scorecard and tracker (Free download available), mastery of the mundane is your secret weapon. With each tick on that scorecard, you're one step closer to your goals—the daily grind, the relentless pursuit that carves the path to your dreams. If you can't measure it, you can't master or improve it. This daily accountability scorecard is one of the bedrock core fundamentals for anyone in business. This is how you attack every day and give yourself or your team the accountability to achieve success.

Download the 100 Point Daily Scorecard Here

Playing the Long Game

My strategy? Play the long game. I've learned the value of patience in a world quick to chase the immediate payout. By offering unparalleled value initially, even at a lower profit, you plant the seeds of a vast, loyal customer base—raving fans who become the loudspeakers of your brand.

Resilience in Adversity

Let's take a moment to dive into the essence of true tenacity. Imagine the unyielding spirit of a Navy SEAL, the relentless courage in the face of sheer adversity. This is the story of Marcus Luttrell and his team, immortalized in the film and book *Lone Survivor.* They embarked on a mission that spiraled into chaos, where every planned move crumbled into dust. Yet, despite the cascading failures, the team's resolve did not falter. Their objective was survival, and with unwavering focus, they navigated through the treacherous landscape, their will to live to burn brighter with each grueling step.

Let's draw a parallel from the battlefield to the economic front lines. Over the past year, industries tied to federal interest rates— real estate, loans, automobile sales—have been through a relentless storm. The professionals who've weathered this storm are the ones who've maintained their resolve, the ones who've continued to stand firm despite the buffeting winds of economic hardship.

However, a disturbing trend emerged when I stumbled upon a post from a mortgage professionals' group. The message? A mere survival strategy suggests that until interest rates deflate, professionals should drive for Uber or DoorDash to tide things over. This struck a nerve. How could seasoned finance professionals advocate for such a passive approach, resigning to circumstances rather than rising above them?

Moreover, the chorus of applause for this "survival strategy" was staggering. It was an anathema to everything I've stood for in the industry. To be a professional in any field is to embody resilience, innovate, and adapt—not surrender to the ebb and flow of market forces.

In my playbook, the approach is vastly different. It's about maintaining the offensive, staying true to your mission, seizing control of what you can influence, and not yielding an inch to external pressures. It's about being the commander of your destiny, not a pawn on the economic chessboard.

So, my dear readers, remember the Seals' tenacity as we navigate these challenging times and let it inspire you. Remember that to attack is not just a burst of action but a sustained campaign, a relentless pursuit of excellence, no matter the battleground you find yourself on. And most importantly, remember that when the going gets tough, the tough gets innovative. Let's set a course for triumph, not just survival. Are you ready to join me in this relentless pursuit?

Step into the arena with me, where excellence is your armor, and external factors are mere shadows that can't touch your steel core. This is where you become so adept at your craft that fluctuations in the world around you become inconsequential background noise. Yes, of course, you pivot and adapt—that's the hallmark of a seasoned warrior, but you do not concede. You do not let go of the reins and hope for eternal salvation. This is the creed of champions, the philosophy of the invincible.

When They Zig... You Zag

Let's talk about the art of making adjustments. It's like a dance—a step back to the basics, a swift pirouette to dodge an unexpected challenge. But it's never about surrendering to the rhythm set by others. It's about orchestrating your music, your moves, and owning the dance floor of your industry.

To attack is to become so immersed in your mission that every fiber of your being is tuned to the frequency of success. It's the obsessive pursuit where the only finish line is victory, and once you cross it, you set up for the next race, hungry for more.

When you're in attack mode, every new dawn is a battle cry, a clarion call to arms. You don't sit idly by, waiting for opportunities to knock. You chase them down; you create them; you become the master of your fate, not a bystander in your own story.

Now, let's get real. This relentless march isn't for the faint-hearted. It's a path less traveled for a reason. If you adopt this battle stance, be prepared to taste failure even more often than success, especially in the early days. But here's the kicker: those perfect weeks and days you'll carve out? They'll become your addiction, the streak you'll chase with the ferocity of a storm.

Imagine setting a goal so tangible, like running a mile every day. It seems simple, but it's a commitment—a promise to yourself. And on the day you stumble, you don't give up because we all stumble. You rise, dust off, and launch the next day with even more zeal.

This brings us to the next chapter in our odyssey: **CONNECTION**. No empire was ever built in isolation, and no legacy was forged alone. As we step into the realm of relationships, understand this: your business, your life's work—it's a collective effort. You need a choir singing your praises to make your business flourish, not just a lone voice. These are your raving fans, your team, your community.

As we pivot to the next chapter (Power of Connection), remember the bridge to success is built on meaningful relationships, not transactional exchanges. So, keep attacking and charging forward with relentless optimism because while not everyone will embark on this journey, you, dear reader, have already taken the first step.

So, as we venture into the realms of **CONNECTION** and beyond, remember this: channel your energies, focus your passion, and let the power of one goal ignite a fire that the world will watch in awe. Are you ready to cast aside the distractions and hone in on your one true goal? Let's pour that water, fill that one cup, and watch as it overflows into a cascade of success. Onward to greatness!

Key Takeaways

1. **Embrace Relentless Networking and Community Engagement**: When I moved to Denver, I showcased the power of attacking from all sides through relentless networking and community engagement. Whether it's running clubs, yoga on the Capitol steps, or beer clubs at night, every interaction is an opportunity to build connections.

Challenge: Identify and immerse yourself in community activities where your presence can make a significant impact and open doors to new opportunities.

2. **Commit Fully to Your Mission**: Attacking your goals requires full commitment. This means segmenting large challenges into manageable tasks and giving your all to each segment, just like the race across Florida.

Challenge: Look at your biggest goal right now. Break it down into smaller, actionable parts and attack each part with full dedication and intensity.

3. **Focus on Mastery of One Thing**: Focus your efforts on mastering one area before expanding to others. Spreading yourself too thin can hinder your growth and success in any single area.

Challenge: Re-evaluate your current projects or goals. Decide on one area where you can channel your focus and efforts to achieve mastery and significant progress.

4. **Embrace the Mundane for Mastery**: Through Lorne's journey and daily sales calls, the narrative underscores the value of embracing and mastering mundane tasks for overall success. Routine and repetition can transform your skills and lead to mastery.

Challenge: Identify one "mundane" task related to your goal that you've been avoiding or underestimating. Commit to practicing this task daily to develop proficiency and excellence.

5. **Resilience in Adversity and the Power of Coaching**: Being resilient, especially in the context of the economic challenges faced by mortgage professionals, emphasizes the importance of maintaining an offensive strategy and the value of coaching and teamwork in overcoming obstacles.

Challenge: Reflect on a current challenge or adversity you're facing. Consider how you can adopt a more resilient and proactive approach to overcome it. Additionally, think about how coaching or teamwork could provide you with the support and perspective needed to persevere.

By embracing these principles of relentlessly attacking—networking, having full commitment, focused mastery, mundane mastery, and resilience in adversity—you can reshape your approach to personal and professional growth. Are you ready to take on these challenges and attack your goals with renewed vigor and strategy?

CHAPTER FIVE

Power of Connection

"Ask and you will receive, seek and you will find, knock and it will be open to you." – Matthew 7:1-10

Join me on a journey through the power of **CONNECTION**—a story of numbers, lives touched, and communities woven tightly through the fabric of engagement and genuine relationships. Imagine standing at the heart of a vast network, where a single conversation can cascade into a wave that reaches thirty thousand lives—and doesn't stop there. Each interaction is a pulse sent out into the world, multiplying as it goes until more millions have felt its rhythm through the digital heartbeat of social media. Let's start with a staggering figure: 30,000. That's the number of individuals I've had the honor to interact with personally. Now, imagine the ripple effect—each person with hundreds, maybe thousands, of connections.

It's a network expanding exponentially, reaching an audience of over fifteen million through social media. In the often dry and dusty realm of mortgage and finance, I've sparked an unexpected interest, creating a buzz where none was expected. Who knew discussions on thirty-year mortgages could ripple out so far and wide? It's a testament to the unyielding power of connection—forging links with others and kindling the fire within.

In the realm of mortgage and finance, an industry not known for viral content, this is a testament to the power of connection. Who would have thought videos about mortgages could capture such attention? We were featured in the September 2023 issue of Inc. Magazine for being a TikTok "influencer" and impacting many lives. But it's not the subject that draws people in; it's the connection forged through the screen, resonating with their lives and aspirations.

The "Why" That Ignites

Let's dive deeper into the essence of connection. It's not just about networking with others but also about connecting to the core of your being, to your "big why." It's a term you've heard, but let's look at it through my mentor, Ben Newman, who discusses connecting with your "burn." It's the fire that fuels your actions, the drive that pushes you through the most challenging times. And if that drive is motivated by wealth, then own it. Money is a tool to create change, influence, and impact.

The world may shy away from admitting a pursuit of money, but not here, not in this narrative of triumph. If money ignites your burn, write it down, shout it from the rooftops, and let it be your beacon through the fog. Embrace your ambitions, whether it's the thrill of driving a luxury car or the goal of becoming a millionaire. It's your journey, your narrative.

Understand that your drive and desires will evolve. What starts as a yearning for a Ferrari may blossom into a passion for philanthropy or innovation. And that's the beauty of growth—an ever-unfolding path that keeps you pushing to new heights.

Now, to the crux of connection: it's about building relationships beyond transactions. It's about creating an authentic community where each interaction is a thread in a larger tapestry. When I started, I practiced what I preached. I reached out, connected, built a business, and thrived on genuine relationships.

Let me share a memory that paints a picture of connection in vivid colors. Imagine me delivering jars of chocolates to clients during the holidays. No sales pitches, just heartfelt wishes and shared smiles. It was a connection in its purest form.

And then there's the power of the handwritten note. It's a practice embedded in my R.A.C.E. Performance Template—writing ten cards daily. It's an art, a personal touch in an increasingly digital world, and it became an anticipated gift, a monthly reminder to my clients that they mattered, that they were more than just a transaction.

In all this, my friends, I became known as the "running realtor," not just for the miles I logged, but for the connections I made along the way. From handing out free dinner cards to engaging with my community, it was about solving problems and providing value beyond expectation.

Solving Problems: The Keys to Growth

So, here's the bottom line: the bigger the problem you solve, the greater the reward. It's not just monetary; it's the satisfaction of making a tangible difference. Finding homes for those with credit challenges or ensuring a better deal is about being a beacon of solutions in a sea of challenges.

As we close this chapter and gear up for the next, remember that connection is the bridge to all successes in life and business. It's the shared journey over the solo sprint. The African proverb rings true: "If you want to go fast, go alone. If you want to go far, go together."

So, take my hand, go far, and build connections that last a lifetime and beyond. Are you ready to connect with the world around you and the fire that burns within? Let's ignite that flame together and watch as the world lights up in response.

The Golden Ticket

As we embark on this delightful exploration of the Power of **CONNECTION**, let's strap in and prepare for a roller coaster of insights that will educate and energize us! Imagine yourself growing, not just in size, but in capability. With growth comes the hefty responsibility of solving larger problems, akin to a video game where each level unlocks a grander challenge and, of course, a more substantial reward—a heftier paycheck. But why play the game? I am going to whisper a secret to success: "With a big enough 'why,' the 'how' doesn't matter." Hold on to that; it's the golden ticket to our journey.

Now, let's dive deep into the ocean of connection. Why, you ask, does it hold the universe together, especially in business? Well, it's the magical ingredient for crafting raving fans—those wonderful beings who become the megaphones for your brand. They're your unpaid, enthusiastic marketers, and in their hands, your brand can either rocket to the stars or sink into oblivion. Free and exponentially powerful word-of-mouth advertising is the old-school "viral" trend.

Consider the titans of the industry: Apple, Nike, Tesla, and Ford. They're not just names but empires that have mastered the art of connection, building legions of loyal fans. These fans would rather walk barefoot over hot coals than switch brands. Apple's followers, for instance, are so devout they might never touch a non-Apple gadget again. It's loyalty not born out of mere satisfaction but of a profound connection to the brand's core values and identity. And Nike, oh, they're not just selling shoes; they're weaving narratives that tug at heartstrings and selling dreams stitched with swooshes. People don't just wear Nike; they wear stories.

But let's pivot to the (non) roaring engines of Tesla and the rugged charm of Ford trucks. They have both cultivated their tribes, yet in wildly unique landscapes—Tesla, with its high-tech allure, and Ford, with its promise of enduring strength. The lesson here is not about the product alone; it's about forging a deep, emotional connection with the audience. It's about becoming an irreplaceable part of their identity.

Then, the plot thickens as we touch upon the power of personal connections. Imagine a world stripped of modern noise—no advertising, no social media, nothing but your reputation. How would you treat that one client in front of you? That treatment, that exceptional experience, is the key to unlocking a network of raving fans.

Our story takes a twist with the mention of COVID-19, a historical juggernaut that reshaped human interaction. Here emerges the protagonist who reached out, fortified old connections, and catered to the community's needs rather than yielding to lockdowns. It's a tale of empathy and resilience that underscores the timeless power of human connection.

The narrative escalates as we discuss proximity to greatness. "You are the sum of the five people you spend the most time with," echoes through the halls of our story. This isn't just a passing comment; it's a strategy for transformation. Our protagonists didn't just bask in the glow of greatness; they sought it, surrounded themselves with it, and absorbed it. From Tony Robbins' events to elite masterminds, the journey was about elevating through association and shared wisdom.

As we near the climax, remember this: **CONNECTING** isn't just a business strategy; it's a life strategy. Staying true to oneself, being disciplined, and **RELENTLESSLY** pursuing the creation of meaningful relationships are the pillars that uphold the temples of success.

As we draw the curtains, if you've made it this far, you're not part of the crowd that gives up easily. You are the **RELENTLESS** executor who doesn't just dream but does. The one who understands that the tapestry of **GREATNESS** is woven with the threads of **CONNECTIONS** made, lessons learned, and actions taken. Now is the moment to turn these words into your reality, to execute with **RELENTLESS** passion, and to create a life of unbelievable **CONNECTIONS** and **GREATNESS**. The stage is set; the audience is waiting; it's time for you to perform.

As we pivot to the next chapter on **EXECUTION**, I challenge you to reflect on the connections you've made and the ones you're yet to forge. Think about the problems you're enthusiastic about solving and how you can turn that passion into a driving force. Are you ready to embrace the challenge and transform your **CONNECTIONS** into a powerful force for success?

Key Takeaways

1. **Harness the Exponential Power of Connection**: My personal interaction with 30,000 individuals and the ripple effect reaching over 15 million through social media exemplifies the vast potential of building and nurturing connections. It's not merely about the numbers but the quality and impact of these interactions that can amplify one's influence and reach.

Challenge: Reflect on your network and consider how you can actively engage and expand it to create a positive ripple effect in your community and beyond.

2. **Identify and Fuel Your "Big Why"**: Connecting deeply with your personal drive or "burn" is essential for sustained motivation and success. Whether it's financial freedom, a passion for helping others, or another goal, acknowledging and embracing this driving force can propel you through challenges.

Challenge: Take a moment to articulate your "big why" and consider how it aligns with your actions and goals. How can you ensure that your daily efforts are fueled by this powerful motivator?

3. **Build Beyond Transactions**: Genuine relationships in business are foundational to creating a community of raving fans and loyal customers. My practice of delivering chocolates to clients and writing handwritten notes emphasizes the importance of personal touches in an increasingly digital world.

Challenge: Identify ways you can add a personal touch to your professional interactions to build deeper, more meaningful relationships beyond mere transactions.

4. **Solve Bigger Problems for Greater Rewards**: The magnitude of problems you solve directly correlates with the rewards you receive. This principle applies not only financially but also to the satisfaction and impact of your work.

Challenge: Evaluate the problems you're currently solving in your professional or personal life. How can you aim higher and tackle more significant challenges to create more considerable value for yourself and others?

5. **Embrace the Power of Proximity and Personal Growth**: Surrounding yourself with individuals who inspire and challenge you can significantly impact your personal and professional development. The narrative underscores the importance of being selective with your inner circle to foster growth and success.

Challenge: Assess your current circle of influence. Consider steps you can take to surround yourself with people who reflect where you want to be, fostering an environment of mutual growth and success.

As you progress to the next chapter on **EXECUTION**, carry with you insights on the power of connection, the clarity of your "big why," the depth of your relationships, the scale of problems you choose to solve, and the influence of your closest circle. Are you ready to apply these principles actively in your journey toward achieving your goals and making a lasting impact?

CHAPTER SIX

Execute, Execute, Execute

"The path to success is to take massive, determined action."
– Tony Robbins

Let's buckle up and sprint through this detailed blueprint of execution that's both a marathon and a sprint, filled with action-packed Saturdays and relentless weekdays. The Symphony of Execution is playing at 5:00 a.m. on a Saturday. While the world slumbers, you sit in solitude, your couch the command center, your laptop the launchpad. With the precision of a maestro, you orchestrate the day's agenda: calls to dial, emails to dispatch, letters to pen. From the quiet of the predawn to the gentle hum of a waking household at 7:00 a.m., you're the early bird plotting the course for the worms you'll catch. As breakfast scents waft through the air, the rest of the house rises, oblivious to the empire you've been building since they last blinked their eyes shut.

At the stroke of eight, you're on the phone. Imagine, for a moment, the ceaseless chatter, the endless dial tones, the symphony of conversations that span three hours. The clock hands dance, and suddenly, you're out the door. Six hours on the battlefield of the real estate market, showing houses, turning dreams into addresses. Can you feel the thrill of each handshake, the hope in each showing? Dragging yourself back home, the contracts await. They don't write themselves, do they?

For another three hours, you pour over paperwork, crafting deals from the day's efforts. But the marathon doesn't end there; another two-hour stretch of follow-ups is the cherry on top of this productivity sundae. This, dear reader, wasn't an anomaly. This was the ritual, the relentless grind, every Saturday for half a decade. It's just one-seventh of the weekly odyssey.

Now, if you think Saturdays were a beast, let's not even start on Monday through Friday—days of equal fervor. And even Sundays, post-church, from one to seven, were no rest days but of restless pursuit of excellence. This relentless, massive action, spanning four to five years, is a testament to the sheer will to execute the plan.

TikTok(ification) of America

Rewind to 2022, a year that stands as a milestone. Picture this: a 50-year-old embarks on a digital odyssey by joining the vibrant world of TikTok. TikTok is the realm of Gen Z, where trends are born and fade within the blink of an eye. The platform wasn't new; it had been around the block, seasoned for three or four years. But for a 50-year-old? It seemed like uncharted territory.

Now, hold that thought. Have you ever stepped into a new world and felt the thrill of the unknown? That was my feeling when the decision was made to dive into TikTok. With a strategic mind, a course was chosen, a path laid out by those who successfully navigated the TikTok waters. Studying was not just reading but absorbing, practicing, and executing. Can you feel the anticipation, the preparation, the ignition of learning?

Fast-forward, and what do you find? Viral success, but not born out of sheer luck or fate. It was a calculated ascent to viral stardom in the mortgage space on TikTok. Millions upon millions of views— think about that—each view a nod of approval, a digital "yes" to the shared content. By 2024, the proof was in the profits, the success standing tall amidst an industry that had seen many falter. ZAP Mortgage didn't just survive; it thrived. When you think of ZAP Mortgage, what do you see? Is it resilience, the innovation, the results?

And yet, there will always be voices of doubt, questioning the "whys" and "hows," not understanding the "whats" and "whens." Why the early mornings? Why the relentless effort? Have you ever felt judged for choosing the less-trodden path?

Let's jog down memory lane to a tale of another who defied norms—Mike Tyson. Why would a champion choose to run at 4:00 a.m.? Because while others are sleeping, champions are working. And if the competition moves the goalposts, say to 3:30 a.m., then so does the champion—to 3:00 a.m. Can you envision that dedication that drives you to be the absolute best?

Mike Tyson, the heavyweight champion, is synonymous with dedication and an unparalleled work ethic. His story isn't just a sports narrative; it's a philosophy that transcends disciplines. It's about the unwavering commitment to outwork, out-train, and outperform the competition. Can you draw parallels to your own life? Where can you push harder, go further, and wake earlier?

So, as you read this, ask yourself: What does it take to achieve greatness in your field? Are you willing to forgo sleep, rise in the silent hours, and train while the world rests? It's not just about physical prowess but about the tenacity of spirit. It's about being the first to rise and the last to retire, the one who turns the improbable into the possible. Are you ready to be that champion in your own life? The journey is demanding, the competition fierce, but the reward is the title "the best." And isn't that worth every 4:00 a.m. alarm?

Housewife to Six-Figures

Let's zoom in and spotlight Rebecka, a paragon of what it means to seize the reins of destiny. Here's Rebecka, whose life intertwines with ours in a serendipitous twist of fate when a simple real estate transaction blossoms into a career-defining pivot. Picture this: She's the spouse of a dedicated military officer, navigating the home-buying journey when their paths cross. They clinch a deal on her first house, and through that process, a rapport is kindled—a connection that's about to catapult her into a whole new echelon.

Fast forward a month, and there's Rebecka on the line, curiosity in her voice, wondering, "What's it like at ZAP Mortgage?" She's in the comfort zone of Wells Fargo, earning a cozy $38,000 annually, remote work's allure keeping her tethered to the home office. She's plugged into the matrix of corporate banking, emails, and calls her daily bread. Yet, despite having the golden key of a license, she's merely orchestrating transactions—important, yet not impactful.

So, when she unveils her salary, there's laughter on the other end—not in mockery, but in the revelation of what's possible. Can you sense her intrigue as she's hit with the reality that her annual earnings were just a couple of days' work for someone else? It's a moment of awakening, the kind that precedes a metamorphosis.

In the ensuing days, they huddle, not just in conversation but in a masterclass of potential. She's shown the very blueprint you're devouring in this book, the same one that has sparked countless success stories. And there's the pivotal question, hanging in the air like a challenge: "Are you ready for this?" Can you feel the weight of that decision, the precipice of change that Rebecka stands upon?

With a resounding yes, she leaps. It's not just a step; it's a quantum jump into massive action in business and life. The transformation is no less than alchemical: from $38,000 to the dizzying heights of six figures. And that's just the beginning. Can you see her trajectory now that she's aiming for the seven-figure summit?

But how does she do it? She taps into her unique world—her sphere. As a military spouse, she wields influence within her community, and her network of friends and acquaintances is fertile ground for her newfound venture. She's not just working a plan; she's living it, breathing it, becoming it.

Play to Win

So, what's the moral here? Decision, commitment, and action are the holy trinity of success. With them, you're invincible; without them, you're just a spectator. Business, this grand, ruthless sport, demands your all. And if you're not playing to win, dominate, or seize that market share, then why play?

You could have the intellect of Einstein, but without execution, it's as good as a dormant volcano—impressive, yet inert. Every day is a match day. The question is, will you step onto the field? Will you engage in the sport of business with the enthusiasm of an athlete, the strategy of a coach, and the heart of a champion? If yes, welcome to the League of Extraordinary Performers, where the game never ends, and neither does the glory. Are you ready to execute, not tomorrow, not after coffee, but now? Because that's where victory lies—in the now. Welcome to the race performance template plan. Let the games begin!

Let's gear up and delve into engineering and entrepreneurship, where the cerebral meets the commercial. Engineering—it's not just about complex calculations and structural designs; it's a field teeming with intellectual giants. As someone with an undergraduate degree in engineering, I can vouch for the smarts it requires. But here's a brain teaser: does being smart equate to business savvy? Not necessarily. As brilliant as they are, engineers often find themselves entangled at a certain echelon within the corporate ladder. Isn't that a conundrum worth pondering?

And yet, intelligence alone doesn't unlock the doors to commercial success. Let's take conference enthusiasts, for instance. Imagine immersing yourself in the electrifying atmosphere of a Tony Robbins event—the pulsing energy, the powerful insights. You could be a repeat attendee or a veteran of self-improvement seminars. But what happens post-conference? Do you find yourself energized but stationary? Why do you think that is?

Let's not mince words—it's all about execution. It's one thing to be a perpetual learner and quite another to be a doer. Have you ever caught yourself marveling at the same faces at these events, year after year, yet they orbit the same spot in their professional universe? They are missing a crucial piece of the puzzle: the execution of gained knowledge.

Now, let's cut to the chase with "The R.A.C.E. Performance Template." This isn't just a planner; it's a blueprint for action. Picture this: a tool that dissects each week of the month, an initial phase followed by a perpetual cycle of growth and achievement. Do you imagine the clarity it could bring to your life?

Download the Race Performance Million Dollar Template Here

But wait, there's more—the daily tracker. It's like having a personal coach in your pocket, keeping you accountable and ensuring you're inching closer to your daily goals. Can you feel the power of daily accomplishments?

Whether you're building a million-dollar enterprise or dreaming bigger—ten million, perhaps?—the devil is in the daily details. It's about doing the little things consistently, every single day. Ever wonder what separates the triumphant from the static? It's the willingness to do what others won't.

Mastery of the "Boring Stuff"

Imagine a relentless consistency in execution, a steadfast commitment to the template, to the tracker. What could that look like for your income, for your life? A tenfold increase? Twenty? Thirty? It's a bold claim, but it's not unfounded. Have you ever heard of a guarantee like that?

The question now is, are you ready to step up to the plate? To swap learning for doing, to transform insights into outcomes? This is your invitation to a year of unparalleled growth. Execute on the template, live by the tracker, and watch your world change. Can you commit to that challenge? The results could be staggering. Welcome to the **EXECUTION** phase—where dreams are forged into reality. Are you in?

Let's break it down and build it up, shall we? When discussing execution, we're not just chatting about your everyday to-do list. We're talking about a commitment to the extraordinary, the stuff that would make even the most stalwart folks balk. Why? Because it's the golden ticket, the secret sauce, the essence that separates the dreamers from the doers. So, are you ready to join the League of Extraordinary Doers?

Picture yourself standing at the edge of a high dive. That's where relentless consistency in the execution phase kicks in—it's the equivalent of not just jumping off that high dive but doing it with a triple somersault and nailing the entry. No splash. Can you see it? That's the precision and dedication we're aiming for. And with this kind of focus, failure is not even in the dictionary. Sure, it's a bold statement, but isn't life all about those bold statements?

Never QUIT

Now, you might wonder how I can drop such a grandiose guarantee that you'll multiply your income by leaps and bounds. Here's the scoop: it's all been road-tested, not in some cushy lab, but in the gritty real-world trenches. Over a decade, hundreds have been handed the keys to the kingdom, this very template and tracker, but guess what? They dropped out. One week in, and poof! Vanished. Why? Because they lacked that relentless spirit, that unwavering commitment. Naysayers and their inner critic swayed them. Have you ever seen a runner stop short of the finish line? That's them.

Now let's talk about the 1%, the cream of the crop, who don't just walk the extra mile; they sprint it. Take the TikTok adventure, for instance. How many 50-year-olds do you see diving into the wild world of TikTok, trying to master the unmasterable? Few, I'd wager. But there I was, learning the ropes, ready to tango with the trendsetters. Why? Because commitment to goals doesn't age discriminate. Are you ready to be that committed?

It's not just about being on social media; it's about leveraging it to catapult your business, touch lives, and spark change on a grand scale. Have you ever thought about the power you hold at your fingertips? With each post and video, you have the potential to alter perspectives to challenge norms. It's a modern-day superpower. Are you willing to wield it?

So, as you march on this execution path, keep your eyes on the prize. It's not just about the activities; it's about the outcome they're driving toward. Tick those boxes, but don't get lost in the minutiae; have you ever caught yourself overthinking to the point of a standstill? That's the "analysis of paralysis" trap. We're not setting that trap today. Instead, we're focusing on the flame within you, that burning desire to achieve what you've set out to do. Can you feel it?

It's about that balance—being laser-focused on the daily actions without losing sight of the bigger picture. Don't just dwell on *What am I going to do today?* Think, *Why am I going to do this today, and how will it take me to where I want to be tomorrow?*

So, tell me, are you ready to execute with the hunger that writes legends? Are you prepared to take your place among the one percent, be relentless, and change lives, including your own? Because that, my friend, is what we're here to do. Let's not just fly; let's soar! Are you in?

Dream Big... Win Big

Embark on a quest, a journey into the vast landscape of your wildest dreams. You're standing at the starting line, eyes fixed on the prize: that elusive million-dollar mark. Or why stop there? Make it one hundred million, two hundred million, even a trillion—let your imagination set the bar. "But how," you ask, "do you bridge the gap from here to there?"

Let's get to the point. Suppose you set your sights on closing 12,000 deals in a single year. Sounds like a mountain of a goal, right? But break it down: 1,000 deals a month, how many per week, how many per day? Can you picture the deals stacking up, one by one, as the days roll by? That's the power of deconstruction. You're not just aiming in the dark but creating a laser-guided path to your target.

The magic happens when you align your daily activities with that grand vision. It's like plotting a treasure map with a big, bold 'X' marking the spot. Every day, you're checking off those boxes, each tick a step closer to the chest of gold. Do you see how the day's victories accumulate, building the momentum that propels you through the weeks, the months, and the year?

Remember, this isn't a sprint; it's a marathon with sprints within it. You won't always cross the finish line first each day, and that's perfectly fine. Perfection is not the goal; progress is. Can you accept the days you don't win, knowing they're just the other side of the coin, the ebb to your flow?

But beware, for the journey is treacherous without discipline. Without a steadfast commitment to your plan, the blueprint meant to uplift you becomes a shackle. Have you ever felt the weight of a plan turned into a burden? Shake it off! Stay riveted on the result, and watch the pieces fall into place like a well-orchestrated symphony.

Let's talk about life's uncertainties, the plates you keep spinning in the air. Have you ever felt like a juggler, plates whirling overhead, a mesmerizing dance of chance and skill? The key, my friend, is to keep those plates aloft, to revel in the uncertainty of it all. Each plate represents a facet of your ambition, and your job is to keep them spinning—because the more you have in the air, the grander the spectacle, the greater the potential reward. Can you handle the pressure, thrive on the adrenaline, and revel in the chaos?

If a plate falls, don't despair. Regroup, refocus, and toss another into the sky. This resilience and comfort with uncertainty forge the steel of success. Are you prepared to juggle with the best of them, to risk a fall in pursuing greatness?

Focus is your wand, your command over energy and growth. Have you heard of Tony Robbins? He's the maestro of this mantra: "Where focus goes, energy flows." Can you channel your focus, harness your energy, and feed it into your dreams? It's all about growth and expansion, setting your gaze on the horizon and marching forward, undeterred.

So, are you ready to commit to the plan, embrace uncertainty, and keep your focus razor-sharp? The day's win is there for the taking. The question is, will you reach out and grab it? Can you live in the exhilaration of the unknown, the thrill of the pursuit, the joy of the journey? Let's set those plates spinning, shall we?

Focus and Discipline

Imagine yourself as the maestro of a grand orchestra, the business world. Each section, from the strings of strategy to the percussion of productivity, plays a critical role. But without your focused direction, the melody can quickly turn into cacophony. So, how do you ensure the symphony soars? It begins with an unyielding focus.

Let's zoom in on this concept of focus. It's like having a supercharged spotlight. When trained on something—bam!—it illuminates every nook and cranny, allowing you to see the potential and the pitfalls. Have you ever seen what happens when you shine a light across a myriad of water cups? A scattered beam brightens many, but none too deeply. Yet, if you spotlight just one cup, it becomes a beacon. That's your business. Can you see it gleaming under the intensity of your focus?

This isn't about being average at many things; it's about being phenomenal at one. When I hit forty or forty-one, the triathlons and marathons had to step aside. Why? Because business became my Ironman. It's a relentless race where the finish line keeps moving. Can you feel that switch flipping, that laser focus channeling into your business?

And here's a little secret: there's no "top in business." It's an infinite climb, a never-ending pursuit of excellence. Are you ready to keep climbing, to reach for the stars, and then some? Think about Michael Jordan and Kobe Bryant. They didn't settle for a handful of rings; they hungered for more. But it wasn't possible without undivided attention to their craft. Can you channel that single-minded pursuit?

Now. I still hit the pavement and feel the rush of the wind as I run because maintaining your health is not optional—it's crucial. It's the fuel that powers your pursuit. But health and hobbies should complement your focus, not compete with it. Are you ready to adjust your lenses to keep the main thing the main thing?

Balance... Not the Same for the 1%

Let's tackle the myth of "balance." Who says you can't have a work-life balance when you're in love with what you do? My work is my play, my business is my hobby, and helping others become millionaires is my passion. Can you say your work is your hobby? Do you find more joy in the thrill of a business win than in binge-watching TV shows? If you're nodding along, you're in the right mindset.

It's about that sweet spot where your work fuels your life, and your life compliments your work. It's about winning, not just in the boardroom, but in life. Can you envision that hundred million, that billion-dollar business, and the next one after that? That's not just success; that's a legacy.

So, we've talked about execution. Now it's time to walk the walk with the R.A.C.E. Performance Template. It's a plan that demands daily, relentless, massive action. Can you commit to that? Can you be someone who doesn't flinch at adversity and meets challenges head-on?

Execution isn't just a piece of the puzzle; it's the cornerstone. Without it, all strategies and systems crumble. Are you ready to be the one who executes flawlessly, turning potential failure into resounding success?

Bringing all the elements of the R.A.C.E framework together is like assembling an elite team, with each member working in harmony. Are you ready to deploy the ultimate strategy for business and life?

This is your moment, the turning point. Will you choose to be the maestro of your destiny, the champion of your own story? Let's make that music. Let's race to the top together. Are you with me? Let's execute.

As we stand on the cusp of culmination, let's take a spirited leap into the essence of our journey: execution. It's the keystone of the R.A.C.E. acronym, the robust core of the Performance System. Why, you may wonder, does execution take such a pedestal? Picture this: Execution is the heartbeat of ambition, the pulse that keeps the dream alive and kicking. Without it, we're merely collectors of ideas, not creators of success.

Be GREAT

Let's face it: nobody wakes up with a burning desire to be mediocre. Failing? Losing? They're not just words but ghosts of potential greatness that never materialized. But you, armed with the power of execution, can ward off these specters. Can you imagine the thrill of conquering each day, of laying your head down each night knowing you're one step closer to your zenith? That's the power of unwavering execution.

Every day presents a crossroads. To quit or to continue? To falter at adversity or to rise above it? With each choice to execute, you're scripting your saga of success. And now, armed to the teeth with every step of the R.A.C.E framework, you're prepared and primed for triumph. Can you feel the synergy as each element (**RELENTLESS, ATTACK, CONNECTION, EXECUTION**) comes together, forming an indestructible alloy to propel you forward?

It's showtime! We're about to orchestrate the grand finale, where each piece of the puzzle slots in to reveal the grand design. Are you ready to witness the alchemy of the R.A.C.E. framework transforming into the ultimate strategy for business and life? Think of it as the most electrifying jigsaw puzzle you've ever solved; each piece is a stepping stone to unparalleled success.

So, take a breath, flex those fingers, and prepare to put it all together. Are you excited to see the picture that emerges when strategy meets action? This isn't just any strategy; it's your strategy, tailor-made for the marathon of business and the sprints of life. Let's turn the page and embark on this final thrilling chapter of creation and mastery. Are you ready to leap from the theoretical to the tangible, from planning to doing, dreaming to being? Let's do this. Let's execute with flair and make the magic happen.

Key Takeaways

1. **Embrace the Early Hours for Unmatched Productivity**: There is an unparalleled productivity and strategic advantage of starting your day before the rest of the world wakes up. Utilizing the early morning hours for planning and executing critical tasks sets a powerful tone for the rest of the day.

Challenge: Consider adjusting your schedule to incorporate early morning work sessions. Experience how these quiet, undisturbed hours can significantly impact your productivity and overall success.

2. **Commit to Relentless, Daily Action**: Success is a product of relentless, consistent action. Be dedicated to executing tasks every day! I executed relentlessly on Saturday, coupled with a rigorous routine on weekdays and even post-church Sundays, which exemplifies a commitment to a relentless pursuit of goals.

Challenge: Identify areas in your life where you can apply a more disciplined, relentless approach. Commit to taking daily actions, no matter how small, towards achieving your goals.

3. **Leverage New Platforms for Growth**: I ventured onto TikTok, a platform predominantly dominated by a younger demographic, underscores the importance of adapting to new technologies and platforms for growth.

Challenge: Explore and embrace new platforms or technologies that may seem outside your comfort zone. Consider how these can be leveraged for personal or professional growth.

4. **Recognize the Power of Specialization**: The success stories shared, including that of Rebecka transitioning from a comfortable salary to earning six figures, emphasize the power of specialization and focusing on one's sphere of influence.

Challenge: Reflect on your own "sphere of influence" and how you can specialize or focus your efforts more effectively within this area to achieve exponential growth.

5. **Execution Overcomes All Obstacles**: Ultimately, the difference between success and failure lies in the ability to execute. The emphasis on executing tasks, regardless of the time or day, serves as a testament to the power of action.

Challenge: Evaluate your current execution strategy. Where can you improve? Set a goal to enhance your execution skills, focusing on discipline, consistency, and resilience in the face of obstacles.

I challenge you to rethink your approach to productivity, adaptability, specialization, and execution. By embracing early mornings, committing to relentless action, leveraging new platforms, focusing on specialization, and prioritizing execution, you can transform your path to success. Are you ready to take on these challenges and elevate your journey to new heights?

CHAPTER SEVEN

The Complete R.A.C.E.

"Things do not change, we do."
– Henry David Thoreau

All right, champions of the corporate coliseum, now that the R.A.C.E. acronym has been demystified, it's showtime! We're not just talking shop here; we're about to craft your millionaire roadmap. Are your engines revved? Good! Because the R.A.C.E. Million Dollar Productivity Template isn't just a tool; it's your new best friend on this wealth quest. Get ready to embrace the grind, the glory, and the gold.

Picture this: a template so finely tuned that it dissects each day, each week, with surgical precision. The initial month is your launchpad, setting the pace and establishing the rhythm. Then, as the weeks roll into months, you're in the groove, building momentum. Can you visualize each tick of the clock, each stroke of the pen, each decision you make adding up to that million-dollar dream?

Now, let's talk strategy and stamina. The magic of this system? Repetition. It's about doing the ordinary to achieve the extraordinary. It's the daily grind, the hustle, the nitty-gritty—yes, it will be as mundane as watching paint dry, but guess what? That paint is going to dry into a masterpiece, your masterpiece. Can you find joy in the monotonous with your eyes on the prize?

This isn't about going through the motions, but mastering them. The template lays out the weekly game plan, but the 100-point-day tracker. That's where accountability meets ambition. It's your coach, accountability partner, and daily dose of "Did I do my best today?" Are you ready to score your success, point by point?

MILLION DOLLAR
PERFORMANCE TEMPLATE

100 POINT DAILY SUCCESS SCORECARD

Name:	Date:
Year Goal: $	Closed: $
Difference: $	Pending: $

Life Points (Separate)	PT Value	Total
Read (30 MIN MINIMUM)	20	
Exercise (30 MIN MINIMUM)	20	
Sex with Spouse (20 MIN)	5	
Total	-	

Task	PT Value	Total
Update CRM	MUST	0
Hours of Power [2 hrs min]	MUST	0
Team Call/Script	5	
Social Media Post	1	
Past Client Touch	1	
Proposal/Offer Made	5	
Coffee Meeting Set	5	
Coffee Appointment KEPT	20	
Sale Made	10	
Sale Closed	15	
Pop By	10	
Text Video Message	2	
Google/ Review	10	
Handwritten Note [sent]	5	
Roleplay	10	
Role Play Extra	15	
Ask For Referral	2	
Zero Email Inbox	5	
Calls (1 Point Each Call)	1	
Total	-	

APPOINTMENTS

1	
2	
3	

NEW CONVERSATIONS

1	2	3	4	5

NURTURES

1	2	3	4	5

SOI

1	2	3	4	5

DIALS

1	2	3	4	5	6	7	8	9	10
11	12	13	14	15	16	17	18	19	20
21	22	23	24	25	26	27	28	29	30
31	32	33	34	35	36	37	38	39	40
41	42	43	44	45	46	47	48	49	50
51	52	53	54	55	56	57	58	59	60
61	62	63	64	65	66	67	68	69	70
71	72	73	74	75	76	77	78	79	80
81	82	83	84	85	86	87	88	89	90
91	92	93	94	95	96	97	98	99	100

SOI LEADS OR YOUR TOP HOT LEADS

1	
2	
3	
4	
5	
6	
7	

100 POINT DAILY SUCCESS SCORECARD

Name:	Date:
Year Goal: $	Closed: $
Difference: $	Pending: $

Life Points (Separate)	PT Value	Total
Read (30 MIN MINIMUM)	20	
Exercise (30 MIN MINIMUM)	20	
Sex with Spouse (20 MIN)	5	
Total	-	

Task	PT Value	Total
Update CRM	MUST	0
Hours of Power [2 hrs min]	MUST	0
Team Call/Script	5	
Social Media Post	1	
Past Client Touch	1	
Proposal/Offer Made	5	
Coffee Meeting Set	5	
Coffee Appointment KEPT	20	
Sale Made	10	
Sale Closed	15	
Pop By	10	
Text Video Message	2	
Google/ Review	10	
Handwritten Note [sent]	5	
Roleplay	10	
Role Play Extra	15	
Ask For Referral	2	
Zero Email Inbox	5	
Calls (1 Point Each Call)	1	
Total	-	

NEW CONVERSATIONS

1	2	3	4	5

NURTURES

1	2	3	4	5

SOI

1	2	3	4	5

DIALS

1	2	3	4	5	6	7	8	9	10
11	12	13	14	15	16	17	18	19	20
21	22	23	24	25	26	27	28	29	30
31	32	33	34	35	36	37	38	39	40
41	42	43	44	45	46	47	48	49	50
51	52	53	54	55	56	57	58	59	60
61	62	63	64	65	66	67	68	69	70
71	72	73	74	75	76	77	78	79	80
81	82	83	84	85	86	87	88	89	90
91	92	93	94	95	96	97	98	99	100

APPOINTMENTS

1	
2	
3	

SOI LEADS OR YOUR TOP HOT LEADS

1	
2	
3	
4	
5	
6	
7	

This tracker isn't a newbie on the block. Oh no, it's been through the wringer since 2015, refined like a diamond to its current state of sparkle and efficiency. And here's the kicker: I can predict your financial future with this tracker with 98% accuracy. Imagine that! How many points will you rack up today? How close are you to that million-dollar melody?

It's time to make the template your own. Tailor it, tweak it, make it fit like a glove for your business. This isn't a one-size-fits-all affair; it's a bespoke suit, ready to be cut to your measurements. Are you prepared to craft your personalized plan of attack?

So, take a deep breath, download that tracker, and let's get to work. The R.A.C.E. is on, and the finish line is flecked with the sparkle of success. Can you commit to the consistency, the relentless action, the daily deeds that will crown you a millionaire? Let's dive in, headfirst, into the ultimate strategy for business and life. Are you game? Let's make it happen, day by day, point by point, until success is not just an option but an inevitable conclusion. On your marks, get set, R.A.C.E.!

Win the Day

All right, it's time to play a game I like to call "Win the Day." The rules? Super simple. Score one hundred points in a day, and you've aced it. That's the baseline, the "good job" pat on the back. It's like the minimum daily requirement but for success. Are you ready to keep score?

Now, let's add a little spice to the game. What happens when you add not one, not two, but three glorious zeros to that one hundred? We're talking 100,000 points over a year. Stay with me here, 365 days, one hundred points a day, and suddenly, you're not just winning the day; you're dominating the year. And the prize? A sweet, six-figure sum nestled in your bank account. Can you feel the excitement?

But hold on because it gets even better. What if you turbocharge your efforts? What if every day you're not just hitting one hundred but 1,000 points on that tracker? Keep that pace for a year, and what do you get? Seven figures, my friend. That's right, a million-dollar payout. Are you seeing the power of points?

However, don't be fooled; this isn't a walk in the park. It's a marathon of sprints, a Herculean effort of epic proportions. The million-dollar question is: Are you up for the challenge? Because when the rubber meets the road, the spreadsheet is open, and the tracker is ticking, you'll see the grit it takes to hit that million-dollar mark.

Everyone wants the millionaire title, but not everyone is cut out for the millionaire hustle. This 100-point day system isn't just a tracker; it's a reality check, a mirror reflecting the effort you need to put in to make those dreams tangible. This system is tried and tested, the secret sauce behind my team members and consulting clients hitting six figures in year one and eyeing the million-dollar prize in years four to five.

So, are you ready to roll up your sleeves and dive into the day-to-day battle that separates the dreamers from the doers, the "wanna-bes" from the "will-bes"? This is your playbook, your step-by-step guide to financial greatness. Will you play the game, chase the points, and turn each tracker tick into a step toward your financial goals? Let's get to it and stack up those points!

Super Lorne

Let's pull back the curtain on a tale that epitomizes the essence of action, the embodiment of the R.A.C.E. framework. This story is about Lorne, a young man whose ambition blazed brighter than a supernova, and it all began at an ordinary cookout where it was a chance meeting with a bunch of physicians and me—a backdrop where destinies can be rewritten.

Then, at a recruiting event at my home, the kind where futures are forged, Lorne approached me. The event was winding down when he said, "Hey, thanks for inviting me. I enjoyed it. I want to join up. I want to sign up." His eagerness was palpable, but could he match the relentless pace of our industry? "Sure," I replied, "here's how you get licensed." But Lorne wasn't about to be a "wait until Monday" kind of guy. "How can I do it now?" he insisted. Can you feel that urgency, that hunger for immediate action?

Lorne's drive didn't just hit the gas; he floored it. He ignited a journey that would typically take months from the embers of Thursday's meeting. By Saturday night, the course was completed. By the following Thursday, he was licensed. Just one week! Are you keeping up? This is a massive action in its purest form.

But wait, Lorne wasn't some carefree soul with time to kill. He was on the precipice of a medical career, in the crucible of med school with residency on the horizon. Debt loomed, but so did dreams—of a debt-free life, a home, a family. "I will outwork you," he challenged me. Have you ever been issued a challenge like that?

We often speak of competition, but this was different. Lorne and I would burn the midnight oil not to outdo each other in mere jest but to embody the spirit of relentless progress—the race template. Lorne didn't just embrace it; he lived it. The 100-point day tracker? He didn't just fill it out; he maxed it out.

Cold calls were his Achilles heel, but did he falter? No, he honed his craft, sharpened his pitch, and turned his weakness into strength. Picture this: Lorne, driving back and forth between Denver and Colorado Springs, not once, not twice, but thrice in a day to seal deals. Can you imagine the mileage, the dedication, the sheer will?

In six months, Lorne didn't just perform; he excelled with the ferocity of a tempest, amassing $300,000 in gross commission income—a staggering $600,000 for the company. How do you measure such effort? It's off the charts. But he wasn't done. Amid this whirlwind, he doubled down, joining me in a workout challenge to prove his mettle in business and personal discipline. Who would emerge with the lowest body fat? It was game on.

Lorne's story is a testament to the boundless potential of the human spirit. His "why" was colossal—debt-free, a home for his family, a secure future secured. His burn wasn't just a flicker but a conflagration that propelled him daily.

So, as we turn the pages from his chapter to yours, ask yourself: What's your cookout moment? What's your massive action? Where's your relentless pursuit? Because if Lorne's story teaches us anything, it's that your limits are narratives waiting to be shattered. Your "why" can fuel your race, and your actions can redefine your reality. Are you ready to make your move? The time is now, and the race is yours to run.

Attention is King

Imagine the bustling marketplace of the business world, where the currency is attention. That's right, attention. It's the most coveted asset, more valuable than gold in the digital age. It's the spotlight that turns a mere whisper into a roar. But is all publicity good publicity? That's debatable. Yet, for the sake of argument, let's say it is. When I took the plunge into TikTok, it wasn't just a dive but a cannonball that sent waves of attention rippling across the digital sea. Can you picture that splash?

But attention alone isn't enough; it's about what you do with it. When I served those with credit scores under 580 to democratize home ownership, it wasn't just business but a revolution. While the crowd zigged, I zagged. Can you feel the thrill of breaking away from the pack?

Now, let's talk about the R.A.C.E. strategy, not just any old race—this was the Grand Prix of strategies, played out on the vast digital stage of TikTok. It's where virality meets strategy, content becomes king, and views crown you as ruler of the digital domain.

Every TikTok drop was like a pebble in a pond, creating ripples that surged through our website traffic. Can you envision the digital dominos falling, one view leading to another, a cascade of clicks and conversions?

Innovation, my friends, is your beacon in the sea of sameness. To stand out, you must dare to be different, to be relentlessly innovative. We're all in sales, but are you just another echo in the chamber, or are you the voice that defines the conversation? When you embrace uniqueness and pair it with relentless execution, what you get isn't growth—it's an explosion.

Create a Legacy

Let's crunch some numbers for a moment. Out of 32.5 million small businesses, imagine catapulting yours to number 294 by 2023. What about climbing to the top twenty of all veteran-owned enterprises in the country? That's not just making a mark; that's etching your name into the annals of business history. Can you see your business soaring to the stratosphere, reaching that rarified 0.0001%?

Yes, we're still the "small business" underdog in the grand scheme, but that's all relative. The stats aren't a boast; they're a beacon, a testament to what's possible when you combine the ingredients in this book with a pinch of audacity and a dash of daring. No background? No problem. No coaching? Who needs it? No experience? It's all the better to write your own rules.

Now, the stage is set for you. What's possible for you? What's your next chapter? Will you grab the reins of the possible and ride into the sunset of success? Your path is waiting, lined with the strategies and stories you've encountered. The next move is yours. What will it be?

Key Takeaways

1. **Embrace the Grind with Precision Planning:** The R.A.C.E. Million Dollar Productivity Template isn't just a tool; it's your strategic partner on the journey to success. It meticulously dissects each day and week, setting a rhythm for your ambitions.

Challenge: How will you incorporate precision planning into your daily routine to ensure every action aligns with your goals?

2. **Find Joy in Repetition (Doing the Boring Stuff):** Success lies in performing ordinary tasks extraordinarily well. The daily grind may seem mundane, but it's in this consistency that greatness is forged.

Challenge: Identify a routine task and commit to mastering it with enthusiasm. How can you transform this task into a stepping stone towards your million-dollar dream?

3. **Accountability Meets Ambition**: The 100-point-day tracker isn't just about tracking tasks; it's about holding yourself accountable to your highest standards.

Challenge: Implement this daily scoring system to measure your productivity and ambition. Reflect on your scores to identify areas for improvement.

4. **Customize Your Path to Success**: True success comes from tailoring the R.A.C.E. template and tracker to fit your unique journey.

Challenge: Personalize your productivity tools to better suit your goals. How will you adjust the template to maximize its effectiveness for your specific aspirations?

5. **Commit to Consistency**: The relentless action and disciplined approach outlined in the R.A.C.E. framework are key to achieving your goals.

Challenge: Evaluate and enhance your commitment to consistent, focused action. Identify where consistency is lacking and take steps to solidify your discipline.

These challenges encourage you to rethink your approach to daily planning, find value in repetition, embrace accountability, personalize your success strategies, and reinforce your commitment to consistency. Are you ready to tackle these challenges head-on and pave your way to success?

The Final Lap

"WINNING IS EVERYTHING."
– Tim Grover

The path to victory, the roadmap to unprecedented success, has been laid before you. It's a path forged not in hope but in action—a blueprint to triumph. Now, the baton is in your hands. It's your turn to sprint forward with veracity and vigor. Remember, history seldom speaks of the runner-up. It's the victor's name that is etched in stone. I urge, challenge, and dare you to take part in life's grand race and win it in every aspect. And how do you win? By living with the urgency of the now, for tomorrow is but a mirage—it's today that counts.

Let's break down the barriers of doubt with two tactical examples—concrete, actionable strategies that make the R.A.C.E. concept universally applicable. It's normal to be skeptical, to think, "Anthony, my business is different." But sit down, let's strategize, and watch the disbelief melt away from your very eyes as possibilities unfold.

Imagine Sally and her candles—a local storefront, an online presence, a physical product yearning for the limelight. This template isn't a vague notion; it's a precision tool. The scalpel transforms a humble candle into a beacon of entrepreneurial spirit. We will delve into this to outline a launch strategy tailored for tangible products and local charm.

Tactical Example #1
Physical Product/Local Store/Online
Using the RACE Template she does the following:

Sally has created the "Ultimate Candle" and has a small shop in her local town and has also created an Etsy page and Shopify store. I used this example of both a retail and online location to prove you can use this template for anything.

RELENTLESS ACTION	CONNECTION EXECUTION
WEEK #1	**WEEK #2**
✓ Send a Video Message with her holding the candle to ALL her contacts	✓ Takes FREE candles to Biz owners she wrote nontes to last week
✓ Call all of her Local Friends	✓ Makes in person and "virtual" coffee appointments with referral sources
✓ Writes handwriitten notes to local business owners that may carry her merchandise	✓ Creates an Email Marketing Campaign and Sends first email with special offer
✓ Joins a Local Business Group/BNI	✓ Finds another meetup networking group to belong to
✓ Creates Affiliate referral program (launches on Social Media)	✓ Creates a monthly "theme" based networking party with her candles i.e.Valentines, easter, halloween etc
✓ Uses the 100 point a day tracker	✓ Scores 250 points/day on tracker

BECOME AN EXPERT AT THE BORING STUFF & MAKE A MILLION DOLLARS	
WEEK #3	**WEEK #4**
✓ Creates a small candle for neighbors within a 1 mile radius and hands them out personally	✓ Write cards for more local business owners and thank you cards
✓ Goes to 5+ in person coffee meetings	✓ Schedule and attend coffees from referrals and friends
✓ Call all out of state contacts and messages all FB friends creating. huge affiliate network	✓ Create pop by tags for next week and increase the amount by 10%/week
✓ Finds another local group to join	✓ Writes and schedules all the emails for next week.
✓ Becomes part of online trade groups on Facebook (add value don't sell)	✓ Starts doing FB/IG live with other local business owners promoting them w/ the candles int eh background
✓ Scores 400 points/day on tracker	✓ Scores 500 on points/day on tracker

You Can Download the PDF Version Here

Now, let's pivot to services—the backbone of our economy. Whether it's real estate, financial advisory, or even the most niche services like gutter cleaning or grill maintenance, this template transcends industries. You could orchestrate the best home car detailing business or reinvent leaf-blowing—this strategy is your golden ticket.

Tactical Example #2
Services Type Business
Real Estate/Mortgage/Insurance/Financial Advisor ETC.

If you are in ANY serviced based industry, it doesn't matter the type. You can apply this template to any business and succeed. This is NOT an all-inclusive list of things to do, but it gives you an idea of where to start. Relentless EXECUTION!!

RELENTLESS	ACTION	CONNECTION	EXECUTION
WEEK #1		**WEEK #2**	

WEEK #1
- Send a Video Message to every single contact just saying hello
- Call all local contacts scheduling coffees. Goal is 30 coffees in 30 days
- Handwritten notes to everyone you know and even people you don't
- Joins a Local Business Group/BNI
- Create Social Media Marketing. plan and. message all FB friends (no more than 49 a day)
- Uses the 100 point a day tracker

WEEK #2
- Takes Pop by gifts to Top 20 clients or people you want as clients
- Takes 10 pop by gifts to referral biz clients.
- Creates an Email Marketing Campaign and Sends first email
- Finds another meetup networking group to belong to
- Plans a date for networking happy hour with biz partners, once a month and everyone invites clients
- Scores 250 points/day on tracker

BECOME AN EXPERT AT THE BORING STUFF & MAKE A MILLION DOLLARS

WEEK #3
- Make brownies or cookies for neighbors within a 1 mile radius and hands them out personally
- Goes to 5+ in person coffee meetings
- Call all out of state contacts and messages all FB friends
- Finds another local group to join
- Become the local "Mayor" go meet business owners and feature them on your FB page
- Scores 400 points/day on tracker

WEEK #4
- Start writing your handwritten notes for next week
- Schedule and attend coffees from referrals and friends
- Create pop by tags for next week and increase the amount by 10%/week
- Writes and schedules all the emails for next week.
- Have your first Networking Happy Hour with Biz Partners
- Scores 500 on points/day on tracker

You Can Download the PDF Version Here

So, you stand at the precipice of action, equipped with the R.A.C.E. performance template, the 100-point day tracker, and illustrative examples to guide your course. The question now is, what will you do with these tools? Will you rise to the occasion? Will you seize this moment to showcase how extraordinary you can be to your family, children, and the world?

As we close this chapter and end this book, your journey is just beginning. And I am here, eagerly awaiting the tales of your triumphs. Engage with the resources at your disposal, visit the online repositories of wisdom at anthonyjlee.com and raceforgreatness.com, and join a community poised for greatness.

Good fortune on your journey—one of courage, determination, and boundless success. Let the R.A.C.E. begin, and see how far you can go.

Acknowledgments

Every milestone reached and every success achieved within these pages has been a journey graced by divine blessing. My heart is full of gratitude to God for bestowing upon me the gifts that have paved my path and for surrounding me with incredible individuals who have made this journey not just possible but deeply meaningful.

To my beloved daughters, Mishayla, Meika, and Toni, your unwavering support and presence have been my constant in every adventure and challenge. Whether it was embracing the thrill of a new quest or patiently sitting through sales calls, your understanding and love have been my anchor. Watching you mature into the remarkable adults you are today fills me with immense pride. I cherish the hope that you will always chase greatness with the same fervor and passion that we've shared in our journey together.

To my cherished grandchildren, Caleb & Logan Wardle, and the little one yet to grace our world, Mishayla's precious unborn child, you represent the bright future of this world. My deepest wish is that two decades from now, as you leaf through these pages, a sense of pride swells within you, knowing your pop-pop was behind these words. You are the beacon of tomorrow, and I hope this book serves as a guide and inspiration for you to carve paths of your own.

My team at Zap Mortgage, your belief in our mission, and your dedication to instigating positive change have been nothing short of inspirational. Your professionalism, integrity, and unwavering commitment exemplify the pinnacle of sales excellence. Together, we've embarked on a mission larger than ourselves, and for that, I am eternally grateful.

Ben Newman, your generosity with your time and wisdom over the years has been a gift. Your incredible foreword and your ongoing commitment to inspiring others across the globe have been a source of constant motivation. Thank you for your mentorship and for being a shining example of what it means to inspire and lead.

To my publishing team at Game Changers Publishing and Cris Cawley, your guidance and expertise have been instrumental in bringing this project to fruition. Your commitment to excellence has transformed this book into something truly special. I am deeply thankful for your partnership and for helping me share my vision with the world.

This book is a testament to the love, support, and faith of each one of you. My journey is richer, and my successes are more meaningful because of your presence in my life. From the bottom of my heart, thank you.

THANK YOU FOR READING MY BOOK!

Here are a few free gifts.

Scan the QR Code Here:

I appreciate your interest in my book and value your feedback as it helps me improve future versions of this book. I would appreciate it if you could leave your invaluable review on Amazon.com with your feedback. Thank you!

Made in the USA
Middletown, DE
17 February 2025

71165774R00079